OFFICE GUIDE TO BUSINESS MATH

W9-CAO-387

OFFICE GUIDE TO BUSINESS MATH

BARBARA ERDSNEKER, M.A.

MACMILLAN • USA

Macmillan General Reference
A Prentice Hall Macmillan Company
15 Columbus Circle
New York, NY 10023

An Arco Book

MACMILLAN is a registered trademark of Macmillan, Inc.
ARCO is a registered trademark of Prentice-Hall, Inc.

Library of Congress Cataloging in Publication Data

Erdsneker, Barbara.
  Office guide to business math / Barbara Erdsneker.
  —2nd ed.
     p. cm.
  ISBN 0-671-89662-8
  1. Business mathematics. I. Title.
HF5691.E655 1994   94-25595
650'.01'513—dc20   CIP

Manufactured in the United States of America

10 9 8 7 6 5 4 3

CONTENTS

TEST YOUR UNDERSTANDING

APPENDIX

WHY USE THIS BOOK?

If numbers have always been your nemesis, this is the book for you. It explains simply and easily how to do every kind of mathematical problem you are likely to face in the performance of your job—from reading large numbers to multiplying and dividing fractions to converting percents and placing decimal points. Each mathematical process is illustrated with step-by-step solutions to the practical problems encountered in the business world.

With this handy reference on your desk you'll never again be at a loss to figure out

- How much overtime pay you are entitled to
- How much you save by paying a bill in 10 days
- How to record checks and reconcile your checking account
- When to place a cross-country phone call
- How to compare mailing costs

and hundreds of other everyday problems.

ARITHMETIC

The Language of Mathematics

In order to solve a mathematical problem, it is essential to know the mathematical meaning of the words used. There are many expressions having the same meaning in mathematics. These expressions may indicate a relationship between quantities, or an operation (addition, subtraction, multiplication, division) to be performed. This chapter will help you to recognize some of the mathematical synonyms commonly found in word problems.

Equality

The following expressions all indicate that two quantities are equal (=):

is equal to	yields
is the same as	gives
the result is	

Addition

The following expressions all indicate that the numbers A and B are to be added:

A + B	**2 + 3**
the sum of A and B	the sum of 2 and 3
the total of A and B	the total of 2 and 3
A added to B	2 added to 3
A increased by B	2 increased by 3
A more than B	2 more than 3
A greater than B	2 greater than 3

Subtraction

The following expressions all indicate that the number B is to be subtracted from the number A:

A − B	**10 − 3**
A minus B	10 minus 3
A less B	10 less 3
the difference of A and B	the difference of 10 and 3
from A subtract B	from 10 subtract 3
A take away B	10 take away 3
A decreased by B	10 decreased by 3
A diminished by B	10 diminished by 3
B is subtracted from A	3 is subtracted from 10
B less than A	3 less than 10

Multiplication

If the numbers A and B are to be multiplied (A × B), the following expressions may be used.

A × B	**2 × 3**
A multiplied by B	2 multiplied by 3
the product of A and B	the product of 2 and 3
A times B	2 times 3

The parts of a multiplication problem are indicated in the example below:

$$
\begin{array}{rl}
15 & \text{(multiplicand)} \\
\times\ 10 & \text{(multiplier)} \\
\hline
150 & \text{(product)}
\end{array}
$$

Division

Division of the numbers A and B (in the order A ÷ B) may be indicated in the following ways.

A ÷ B	14 ÷ 2
A divided by B	14 divided by 2
the quotient of A and B	the quotient of 14 and 2

The parts of a division problem are indicated in the example below:

$$\begin{array}{r} 5\frac{1}{7} \\ 7\overline{)36} \\ 35 \\ \hline 1 \end{array}$$

(divisor) (quotient) (dividend) (remainder)

Factors and Divisors

The relationship A × B = C, for any whole numbers A, B, and C, may be expressed as:

A × B = C	2 × 3 = 6
A and B are factors of C	2 and 3 are factors of 6
A and B are divisors of C	2 and 3 are divisors of 6
C is divisible by A and by B	6 is divisible by 2 and by 3
C is a multiple of A and of B	6 is a multiple of 2 and of 3

Whole Numbers

Place Value

1. The value of each digit in a whole number depends on the column in which it appears.

Example:

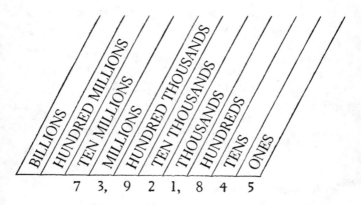

7 3, 9 2 1, 8 4 5

In the number 73,921,845 the 2 is in the ten thousands column and has the value 2 ten thousands, or 20,000. The 3 is in the millions column and has the value 3 millions, or 3,000,000.

Reading Large Numbers

2. To read a large number in words, first use commas to separate the digits into groups of three, starting from the right. Then read each group from left to right.

   Example: 73,921,845 is read "seventy-three million, nine hundred twenty-one thousand, eight hundred forty-five." In this example, 73 is in the millions group, 921 is in the thousands group, and 845 is in the ones group (although the word *ones* is not read).

Example: 6,305,009,802 is read "six billion, three hundred five million, nine thousand, eight hundred two." The 6 is in the billions group, the 305 is in the millions group, the 009 is in the thousands group, and the 802 is in the ones group.

Number Facts

3. In order to add, subtract, multiply, or divide any numbers easily, you must know the basic number facts for whole numbers. These may be found in the following addition and multiplication tables.

ADDITION FACTS

+	0	1	2	3	4	5	6	7	8	9
0	0	1	2	3	4	5	6	7	8	9
1	1	2	3	4	5	6	7	8	9	10
2	2	3	4	5	6	7	8	9	10	11
3	3	4	5	6	7	8	9	10	11	12
4	4	5	6	7	8	9	10	11	12	13
5	5	6	7	8	9	10	11	12	13	14
6	6	7	8	9	10	11	12	13	14	15
7	7	8	9	10	11	12	13	14	15	16
8	8	9	10	11	12	13	14	15	16	17
9	9	10	11	12	13	14	15	16	17	18

MULTIPLICATION FACTS

×	0	1	2	3	4	5	6	7	8	9
0	0	0	0	0	0	0	0	0	0	0
1	0	1	2	3	4	5	6	7	8	9
2	0	2	4	6	8	10	12	14	16	18
3	0	3	6	9	12	15	18	21	24	27
4	0	4	8	12	16	20	24	28	32	36
5	0	5	10	15	20	25	30	35	40	45
6	0	6	12	18	24	30	36	42	48	54
7	0	7	14	21	28	35	42	49	56	63
8	0	8	16	24	32	40	48	56	64	72
9	0	9	18	27	36	45	54	63	72	81

Addition

4. To add whole numbers, columns should be lined up, starting with the ones column. Add one column at a time, carrying to the next column to the left whenever necessary.

   Example: Add 63 + 194 + 5 + 1067.

Solution:

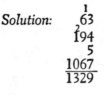

> Note that the 3,4,5, and 7 are all in the ones column.
>
> A 1 has been carried to the tens column and a 2 has been carried to the hundreds column.

Subtraction

5. When subtracting, as in adding, like columns must be lined up. Subtract each column starting from the ones column, and if necessary borrow from the next column to the left.

   Example: Subtract 8930 − 5426.

   Solution:
   $$\begin{array}{r} {}^{2\,1}89\overset{}{3}0 \\ -\,5426 \\ \hline 3504 \end{array}$$

   > Note that 1 was borrowed from the 3 in the tens column.

   Example: Subtract 49 from 407.

   Solution:
   $$\begin{array}{r} {}^{3\,9\,1}40\overset{}{7} \\ -\ \ 49 \\ \hline 358 \end{array}$$

   > In order to borrow from the tens column, it was first necessary to borrow from the hundreds column.

Multiplication

6. To multiply by a one-digit number, multiply each digit of the multiplicand by the multiplier, carrying where necessary.

Example: Multiply 842 by 3.

Solution:
```
      1
    842        Notice the 1 carried to
  ×   3        the hundreds column:
   2526            3 × 8 = 24
                  24 + 1 = 25
```

7. To multiply by a number which has more than one digit, multiply each digit of the multiplicand by each digit of the multiplier, then add the partial products.

Example: Multiply 154 × 73.
Solution:
```
    154
  × 73
    462        3 × 154 =  462
   1078        7 × 154 = 1078
  11242        The 8 is placed in the
               same column as the 7 of
               73.
```

Example: Multiply 2603 × 518.
Solution:
```
     2603
   ×  518
    20824      8 × 2603 = 20824
     2603      1 × 2603 = 2603
    13015      5 × 2603 = 13015
  1348354          Add the partial
                   products.
```

Notice that when multiplying by the digit in the ones column, the first digit of the product is placed in the ones column (see the 4 in 20824). When multiplying by the digit in the tens column (1), the first digit of the product is placed in the tens column. When multiplying by the digit in the hundreds column (5), the first digit of the product is placed in the hundreds column (see the 5 in 13015).

Division

8. Division is a process of estimating, multiplying to check that estimate, and subtracting.

Example: Divide 7461 by 3.
Solution:
There are about 2000 threes in 7461. It is easiest to think of there being 2 threes in 7, and placing the 2 in the thousands place.
Multiply $2 \times 3 = 6$
Subtract $7 - 6 = 1$, then bring down the 4.
Estimate that there are about 4 threes in 14.
Multiply $3 \times 4 = 12$
Subtract $14 - 12 = 2$, then bring down the 6.
There are about 8 threes in 26.
Multiply $8 \times 3 = 24$
Subtract $26 - 24 = 2$
Bring down the 1.
There are 7 threes in 21.
Multiply $7 \times 3 = 21$
Subtract $21 - 21 = 0$
There is no remainder.

$$\begin{array}{r} 2487 \\ 3\overline{)7461} \\ \underline{6} \\ 14 \\ \underline{12} \\ 26 \\ \underline{24} \\ 21 \\ \underline{21} \\ 0 \end{array}$$

Example: $420 \div 35$

Solution:
```
      12
35)420
      35|
      70
      70
       0
```
There is 1 thirty-five in 42.
Place the 1 in the same column as the 2 of 42.
Multiply $1 \times 35 = 35$
Subtract $42 - 35 = 7$
Bring down the 0.
There are 2 thirty-fives in 70. $2 \times 35 = 70$
$70 - 70 = 0$

Example: Divide 2759 by 81.

Solution:
```
       34
81)2759
      243|
      329
      324
        5
```
There are about 3 eighty-ones in 275.
$3 \times 81 = 243$
$275 - 243 = 32$
Bring down the 9.
There are about 4 eighty-ones in 329.
$4 \times 81 = 324$
$329 - 324 = 5$
The remainder is 5.

The answer may be written as 34 remainder 5, or as 34⅚₁, with the remainder placed over the divisor.

Fractions

Fractions and Mixed Numbers

1. A fraction is part of a unit.

   a. A fraction has a numerator and a denominator.

Example: In the fraction ¾, 3 is the numerator and 4 is the denominator.

b. In any fraction, the numerator is being divided by the denominator.

Example: The fraction 2/7 indicates that 2 is being divided by 7.

c. In a fraction problem, the whole quantity is 1, which may be expressed by a fraction in which the numerator and denominator are the same number.

Example: If the problem involves ⅛ of a quantity, then the whole quantity is ⅛, or 1.

2. A **mixed number** is an integer together with a fraction, such as 2⅗, 7⅜, etc. The integer is the integral part, and the fraction is the fractional part.

3. An **improper fraction** is one in which the numerator is equal to or greater than the denominator, such as ¹⁹⁄₆, ²⁵⁄₄, or ¹⁰⁄₁₀.

4. To change a mixed number to an improper fraction:

a. Multiply the denominator of the fraction by the integer.

b. Add the numerator to this product.

c. Place this sum over the denominator of the fraction.

Example: Change 3½ to an improper fraction.

Solution: $7 \times 3 = 21$
$21 + 4 = 25$
$3\frac{4}{7} = \frac{25}{7}$

5. To change an improper fraction to a mixed number:

   a. Divide the numerator by the denominator. The quotient, disregarding the remainder, is the integral part of the mixed number.

   b. Place the remainder, if any, over the denominator. This is the fractional part of the mixed number.

Example: Change $\frac{36}{13}$ to a mixed number.
Solution:

$$13\overline{)36} \atop $$

$$\begin{array}{r} 2 \\ 13\overline{)36} \\ 26 \\ \hline 10 \quad \text{remainder} \end{array}$$

$\frac{36}{13} = 2\frac{10}{13}$

6. The numerator and denominator of a fraction may be changed by multiplying both by the same number, without affecting the value of the fraction.

   Example: The value of the fraction $\frac{2}{5}$ will not be altered if the numerator and the denominator are multiplied by 2, to result in $\frac{4}{10}$.

7. The numerator and the denominator of a fraction may be changed by dividing both by the same number, without affecting the value of the fraction. This process is called **reducing the fraction**. A fraction that has been reduced as much as possible is said to be in **lowest terms**.

Example: The value of the fraction ³⁄₁₂ will not be altered if the numerator and denominator are divided by 3, to result in ¼.

Example: If ⁶⁄₃₀ is reduced to lowest terms (by dividing both numerator and denominator by 6), the result is ⅕.

8. As a final answer to a problem:

   a. Improper fractions should be changed to mixed numbers.

   b. Fractions should be reduced as far as possible.

Addition

9. Fractions cannot be added unless the denominators are all the same.

   a. If the denominators are the same, add all the numerators and place this sum over the common denominator. In the case of mixed numbers, follow the above rule for the fractions and then add the integers.

   Example: The sum of 2⅜ + 3⅛ + ⅜ = 5⅞

   b. If the denominators are not the same, the fractions, in order to be added, must be converted to ones having the same denominator. To do this, it is first necessary to find the lowest common denominator.

10. The **lowest common denominator** (henceforth called the L.C.D.) is the lowest number that can be divided evenly by all the given denominators. If no

two of the given denominators can be divided by the same number, then the L.C.D. is the product of all the denominators.

Example: The L.C.D. of $\frac{1}{2}$, $\frac{1}{3}$, and $\frac{1}{5}$ is

$$2 \times 3 \times 5 = 30$$

11. To find the L.C.D. when two or more of the given denominators can be divided by the same number:

 a. Write down the denominators, leaving plenty of space between the numbers.

 b. Select the smallest number (other than 1) by which one or more of the denominators can be divided evenly.

 c. Divide the denominators by this number, copying down those that cannot be divided evenly. Place this number to one side.

 d. Repeat this process, placing each divisor to one side until there are no longer any denominators that can be divided evenly by any selected number.

 e. Multiply all the divisors to find the L.C.D.

Example: Find the L.C.D. of $\frac{1}{5}$, $\frac{1}{7}$, $\frac{1}{10}$, and $\frac{1}{14}$.

Solution:

2)	5	7	10	14
5)	5	7	5	7
7)	1	7	1	7
	1	1	1	1

$$7 \times 5 \times 2 = 70$$

The L.C.D. is 70

12. To add fractions having different denominators:
   a. Find the L.C.D. of the denominators.
   b. Change each fraction to an equivalent fraction having the L.C.D. as its denominator.
   c. When all of the fractions have the same denominator, they may be added, as in the example following item 9a.

Example: Add $\frac{1}{4}$, $\frac{3}{10}$, and $\frac{2}{5}$.
Solution: Find the L.C.D.:

$$
\begin{array}{r|lll}
2)4 & 10 & 5 \\
2)2 & 5 & 5 \\
5)1 & 5 & 5 \\
1 & 1 & 1
\end{array}
$$

L.C.D. $= 2 \times 2 \times 5 = 20$

$$
\begin{aligned}
\frac{1}{4} &= \frac{5}{20} \\
\frac{3}{10} &= \frac{6}{20} \\
+ \frac{2}{5} &= + \frac{8}{20} \\
\hline
&\quad \frac{19}{20}
\end{aligned}
$$

13. To add mixed numbers in which the fractions have different denominators, add the fractions by following the rules in item 12 above, then add the integers.

Example: Add $2\frac{5}{7}$, $5\frac{1}{2}$, and 8.
Solution: L.C.D. $= 14$

$$
\begin{aligned}
2\frac{5}{7} &= 2\frac{10}{14} \\
5\frac{1}{2} &= 5\frac{7}{14} \\
+8 &= + 8 \\
\hline
&\quad 15\frac{17}{14} = 16\frac{3}{14}
\end{aligned}
$$

Subtraction

14. a. Unlike addition, which may involve adding more than two numbers at the same time, subtraction involves only two numbers.

    b. In subtraction, as in addition, the denominators must be the same.

15. To subtract fractions:

    a. Find the L.C.D.

    b. Change both fractions so that each has the L.C.D. as the denominator.

    c. Subtract the numerator of the second fraction from the numerator of the first, and place this difference over the L.C.D.

    d. Reduce, if possible.

    Example: Find the difference of ⅝ and ¼.
    Solution: L.C.D. =   8

$$
\begin{array}{rr}
\frac{5}{8} = & \frac{5}{8} \\
- \frac{1}{4} = & - \frac{2}{8} \\
\hline
& \frac{3}{8}
\end{array}
$$

16. To subtract mixed numbers:

    a. It may be necessary to "borrow," so that the fractional part of the first term is larger than the fractional part of the second term.

    b. Subtract the fractional parts of the mixed numbers and reduce.

    c. Subtract the integers.

Example: Subtract 16⅕ from 29⅓.
Solution: L.C.D. =   15

$$29\tfrac{1}{3} = 29\tfrac{5}{15}$$
$$- 16\tfrac{1}{5} = - 16\tfrac{12}{15}$$

Note that ⁵⁄₁₅ is less than ¹²⁄₁₅. Borrow 1 from 29, and change to ¹⁵⁄₁₅.

$$29\tfrac{5}{15} = 28\tfrac{20}{15}$$
$$- 16\tfrac{12}{15} = - 16\tfrac{12}{15}$$
$$\overline{12\tfrac{8}{15}}$$

Multiplication

17.   a. To be multiplied, fractions need not have the same denominators.

    b. A whole number has the denominator 1 understood.

18.   To multiply fractions:

    a. Change the mixed numbers, if any, to improper fractions.

    b. Multiply all the numerators, and place this product over the product of the denominators.

    c. Reduce, if possible.

Example: Multiply ⅔ × 2⁴⁄₇ × ⁵⁄₉.
Solution: 2⁴⁄₇ = ¹⁸⁄₇
$$\tfrac{2}{3} \times \tfrac{18}{7} \times \tfrac{5}{9} = \tfrac{180}{189}$$
$$= \tfrac{20}{21}$$

19. a. Cancellation is a device to facilitate multiplication. To cancel means to divide a numerator and a denominator by the same number in a multiplication problem.

Example: In the problem $\frac{4}{7} \times \frac{5}{6}$, the numerator **4** and the denominator 6 may be divided by 2.

$$\frac{\overset{2}{4}}{7} \times \frac{5}{\underset{3}{6}} = \frac{10}{21}$$

b. The word "of" is often used to mean "multiply."

Example: ½ of ½ = ½ × ½ = ¼

20. To multiply a whole number by a mixed number:

a. Multiply the whole number by the fractional part of the mixed number.

b. Multiply the whole number by the integral part of the mixed number.

c. Add both products.

Example: Multiply 23¾ by 95.
Solution: $\frac{95}{1} \times \frac{3}{4} = \frac{285}{4}$
                              $= 71\frac{1}{4}$
                $95 \times 23 = 2185$
        $2185 + 71\frac{1}{4} = 2256\frac{1}{4}$

Division

21. The **reciprocal** of a fraction is that fraction inverted.

a. When a fraction is inverted, the numerator becomes the denominator and the denominator becomes the numerator.

Example: The reciprocal of $3/8$ is $8/3$.
Example: The reciprocal of $1/3$ is $3/1$, or simply 3.

b. Since every whole number has the denominator 1 understood, the reciprocal of a whole number is a fraction having 1 as the numerator and the number itself as the denominator.

Example: The reciprocal of 5 (expressed fractionally as $5/1$) is $1/5$.

22. To divide fractions:

a. Change all the mixed numbers, if any, to improper fractions.

b. Invert the second fraction and multiply.

c. Reduce, if possible.

Example: Divide $2/3$ by $2\frac{1}{4}$.
Solution:

$$2\tfrac{1}{4} = 9/4$$
$$2/3 \div 9/4 = 2/3 \times 4/9$$
$$= 8/27$$

23. A **complex fraction** is one that has a fraction as the numerator, or as the denominator, or as both.

Example: $\frac{2/3}{5}$ is a complex fraction.

24. To clear (simplify) a complex fraction:

a. Divide the numerator by the denominator.

b. Reduce, if possible.

Example: Clear $\frac{3/7}{5/14}$.

Solution: $3/7 \div 5/14 = 3/7 \times 14/5 = {}^{42}/_{35}$
$= {}^6/_5$
$= 1\frac{1}{5}$

Comparing Fractions

25. If two fractions have the same denominator, the one having the larger numerator is the greater fraction.

    Example: $3/7$ is greater than $2/7$.

26. If two fractions have the same numerator, the one having the larger denominator is the smaller fraction.

    Example: $5/12$ is smaller than $5/11$.

27. To compare two fractions having different numerators and different denominators:

    a. Change the fractions to equivalent fractions having their L.C.D. as their new denominator.

    b. Compare, as in the example following item 25.

Example: Compare $4/7$ and $5/8$.
Solution: L.C.D. $= 7 \times 8 = 56$
$4/7 = {}^{32}/_{56}$
$5/8 = {}^{35}/_{56}$

Since ${}^{35}/_{56}$ is larger than ${}^{32}/_{56}$, $5/8$ is larger than $4/7$.

Fraction Problems

28. Most fraction problems can be arranged in the form: "What fraction of a number is another number?" This form contains three important parts:

- The fractional part
- The number following "of"
- The number following "is"

a. If the fraction and the "of" number are given, multiply them to find the "is" number.

Example: What is ¾ of 20?
Solution: Write the question as "¾ of 20 is what number?" Then multiply the fraction ¾ by the "of" number, 20:

$$\frac{3}{\underset{1}{4}} \times \overset{5}{20} = 15$$

b. If the fractional part and the "is" number are given, divide the "is" number by the fraction to find the "of" number.

Example: ⅘ of what number is 40?
Solution: To find the "of" number, divide 40 by ⅘:

$$40 \div \frac{4}{5} = \overset{10}{\underset{1}{\cancel{40}}}/1 \times \frac{5}{\underset{1}{\cancel{4}}}$$
$$= 50$$

c. To find the fractional part when the other two numbers are known, divide the "is" number by the "of" number

Example: What part of 12 is 9?
Solution: $9 \div 12 = \frac{9}{12}$
$= \frac{3}{4}$

Decimals

Place Value

1. a. As with whole numbers, each digit in a decimal
    number has a value that depends on the column
    in which it appears.

    Example:

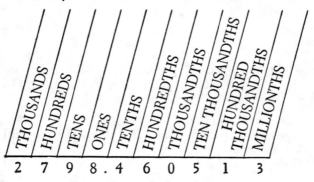

The decimal point separates the ones column
from the tenths column.
In the number 2798.460513, the 5 has the value
5 ten thousandths, or $\frac{5}{10,000}$. The 6 has the value 6
hundredths, or $\frac{6}{100}$.

b. The decimal number is actually a fraction with a denominator in the power of 10. The number of digits, or places, after a decimal point determines which power of 10 the denominator is. If there is one digit, the denominator is understood to be 10; if there are two digits, the denominator is understood to be 100, etc.

Example: $.3 = \frac{3}{10}$, $.57 = \frac{57}{100}$, $.643 = \frac{643}{1000}$

c. The decimal part of a number is read as a whole number followed by the value of the smallest place.

Example: .2385 is read "two thousand, three hundred eighty-five ten thousandths" since the smallest decimal place is ten thousandths.

Example: 63.904 is read "sixty-three and nine hundred four thousandths." The word "and" indicates the decimal point.

d. The addition of zeros after a decimal point does not change the value of the decimal. The zeros may be removed without changing the value of the decimal.

Example: $.7 = .70 = .700$ and vice versa, $.700 = .70 = .7$

e. Since a decimal point is understood to exist after any whole number, the addition of any number of zeroes after such a decimal point does not change the value of the number.

Example: $2 = 2.0 = 2.00 = 2.000$

Addition

2. Decimals are added in the same way that whole numbers are added, with the provision that the decimal points must be kept in a vertical line, one under the other. This determines the place of the decimal point in the answer.

Example: Add 2.31, .037, 4, and 5.0017.
Solution:

```
      2.3100
       .0370
      4.0000
  +   5.0017
     11.3487
```

Subtraction

3. Decimals are subtracted in the same way that whole numbers are subtracted, with the provision that, as in addition, the decimal points must be kept in a vertical line, one under the other. This determines the place of the decimal point in the answer.

Example: Subtract 4.0037 from 15.3.
Solution:

```
     15.3000
  -   4.0037
     11.2963
```

Multiplication

4. Decimals are multiplied in the same way that whole numbers are multiplied.

   a. The number of decimal places in the product equals the sum of the decimal places in the multiplicand and in the multiplier.

b. If there are fewer places in the product than this sum, then a sufficient number of zeros must be added in front of the product to equal the number of places required, and a decimal point is written in front of the zeros.

Example: Multiply 2.372 by .012.
Solution:

$$
\begin{array}{r}
2.372 \quad \text{(3 decimal places)} \\
\times \quad .012 \quad \text{(3 decimal places)} \\
\hline
4744 \\
2372 \\
\hline
.028464 \quad \text{(6 decimal places)}
\end{array}
$$

5. A decimal can be multiplied by a power of 10 by moving the decimal point to the *right* as many places as indicated by the power. If multiplied by 10, the decimal point is moved one place to the right; if multiplied by 100, the decimal point is moved two places to the right; etc.

Example:
$$.235 \times 10 \ = \ 2.35$$
$$.235 \times 100 \ = \ 23.5$$
$$.235 \times 1000 = 235$$

Division

6. There are four types of division involving decimals:
   - When the dividend only is a decimal
   - When the divisor only is a decimal
   - When both are decimals
   - When neither dividend nor divisor is a decimal

   a. When the dividend only is a decimal, the division is the same as that of whole numbers, except that a decimal point must be placed in the quotient exactly above that in the dividend.

Example: Divide 12.864 by 32.
Solution:

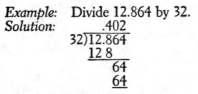

```
        .402
  32)12.864
     12 8
        64
        64
```

b. When the divisor only is a decimal, the decimal point in the divisor is omitted and as many zeros are placed to the right of the dividend as there were decimal places in the divisor.

Example: Divide 211327 by 6.817.
Solution:

```
                          31000  (3 zeros added)
  6.817)211327 = 6817)211327000
  (3 deci-                20451
    mal places)            6817
                           6817
```

c. When both divisor and dividend are decimals, the decimal point in the divisor is omitted and the decimal point in the dividend must be noved to the right as many decimal places as there were in the divisor. If there are not enough places in the dividend, zeros must be added to make up the difference.

Example: Divide 2.62 by .131.

Solution:

```
                    20
  .131)2.62 = 131)2620
                   262
```

d. In instances when neither the divisor nor the dividend is a decimal, a problem may still in-

volve decimals. This occurs in two cases: when
the dividend is a smaller number than the divisor; and when it is required to work out a division to a certain number of decimal places. In
either case, write in a decimal point after the
dividend, add as many zeros as necessary, and
place a decimal point in the quotient above that
in the dividend.

Example: Divide 7 by 50.

```
           .14
Solution:  50)7.00
             5 0
             2 00
             2 00
```

Example: How much is 155 divided by 40, carried
out to 3 decimal places?

```
            3.875
Solution:  40)155.000
              120
               35 0
               32 0
                3 00
                2 80
                  200
```

7. A decimal can be divided by a power of 10 by moving the decimal to the *left* as many places as indicated by the power. If divided by 10, the decimal
point is moved one place to the left; if divided by
100, the decimal point is moved two places to the
left; etc. If there are not enough places, add zeros in
front of the number to make up the difference and
add a decimal point.

Example: .4 divided by 10 = .04
.4 divided by 100 = .004

Rounding Decimals

8. To round a number to a given decimal place:

   a. Locate the given place.

   b. If the digit to the right is less than 5, omit all digits following the given place.

   c. If the digit to the right is 5 or more, raise the given place by 1 and omit all digits following the given place.

   Examples: 4.27 = 4.3 to the nearest tenth
   .71345 = .713 to the nearest thousandth

9. In problems involving money, answers are usually rounded to the nearest cent.

Conversion of Fractions to Decimals

10. A fraction can be changed to a decimal by dividing the numerator by the denominator and working out the division to as many decimal places as required.

    Example: Change $\frac{5}{11}$ to a decimal of 2 places.

    Solution: $\frac{5}{11} = 11\overline{)5.00}$ .45$\frac{5}{11}$
    $\underline{4.44}$
    60
    $\underline{55}$
    5

11. To clear fractions containing a decimal in either the numerator or the denominator, or in both, divide the numerator by the denominator.

Example: What is the value of $\frac{2.34}{.6}$?

Solution: $\frac{2.34}{.6} = .6\overline{)2.34} = 6\overline{)23.4}$

$$
\begin{array}{r}
3.9 \\
6\overline{)23.4} \\
\underline{18} \\
5\,4 \\
\underline{5\,4}
\end{array}
$$

Conversion of Decimals to Fractions

12. Since a decimal point indicates a number having a denominator that is a power of 10, a decimal can be expressed as a fraction, the numerator of which is the number itself and the denominator of which is the power indicated by the number of decimal places in the decimal.

Example: $.3 = \frac{3}{10}$, $.47 = \frac{47}{100}$

13. When the decimal is a mixed number, divide by the power of 10 indicated by its number of decimal places. The fraction does not count as a decimal place.

Example: Change $.25\frac{1}{3}$ to a fraction.
Solution: $.25\frac{1}{3} = 25\frac{1}{3} \div 100$
$= \frac{76}{3} \times \frac{1}{100}$
$= \frac{76}{300} = \frac{19}{75}$

14. When to change decimals to fractions:
   a. When dealing with whole numbers, do not change the decimal.

Example: In the problem 12 × .14, it is better to keep the decimal:

$$12 \times .14 = 1.68$$

b. When dealing with fractions, change the decimal to a fraction.

Example: In the problem ⅗ × .17, it is best to change the decimal to a fraction:

$$⅗ \times .17 = ⅗ \times {}^{17}\!/_{100} = {}^{51}\!/_{500}$$

15. Because decimal equivalents of fractions are often used, it is helpful to be familiar with the most common conversions.

½ = .5	⅓ = .3333
¼ = .25	⅔ = .6667
¾ = .75	⅙ = .1667
⅕ = .2	1/7 = .1429
⅛ = .125	1/9 = .1111
1/16 = .0625	1/12 = .0833

Note that the left column contains exact values. The values in the right column have been rounded to the nearest ten-thousandth.

Percents

1. The percent symbol (%) means "parts of a hundred." Some problems involve expressing a fraction or a decimal as a percent. In other problems, it is necessary to express a percent as a fraction or a decimal in order to perform the calculations.

Conversions

2. To change a whole number or a decimal to a percent:

   a. Multiply the number by 100.

   b. Affix a % sign.

   Example: Change 3 to a percent.
   Solution: $3 \times 100 = 300$
   $$3 = 300\%$$

   Example: Change .67 to a percent.
   Solution: $.67 \times 100 = 67$
   $$.67 = 67\%$$

3. To change a fraction or a mixed number to a percent:

   a. Multiply the fraction or mixed number by 100.

   b. Reduce, if possible.

   c. Affix a % sign.

   Example: Change ½ to a percent.
   Solution: $\frac{1}{2} \times 100 = \frac{100}{2}$
   $$= 14\frac{2}{7}$$
   $$\frac{1}{7} = 14\frac{2}{7}\%$$

   Example: Change 4⅔ to a percent.
   Solution: $4\frac{2}{3} \times 100 = \frac{14}{3} \times 100 = \frac{1400}{3}$
   $$= 466\frac{2}{3}$$
   $$4\frac{2}{3} = 466\frac{2}{3}\%$$

4. To remove a % sign attached to a decimal, divide the decimal by 100. If necessary, the resulting decimal may then be changed to a fraction.

Example: Change .5% to a decimal and to a fraction.
Solution: .5% = .5 ÷ 100 = .005
.005 = ⁵⁄₁₀₀₀ = ½₀₀

5. To remove a % sign attached to a fraction or mixed number, divide the fraction or mixed number by 100, and reduce, if possible. If necessary, the resulting fraction may then be changed to a decimal.

Example: Change ¾% to a fraction and to a decimal.
Solution: ¾% = ¾ ÷ 100 = ¾ × ¹⁄₁₀₀
= ³⁄₄₀₀

$$\frac{3}{400} = 400\overline{)3.0000} \quad .0075$$

6. To remove a % sign attached to a decimal that includes a fraction, divide the decimal by 100. If necessary, the resulting number may then be changed to a fraction.

Example: Change .5⅓% to a fraction.
Solution: .5⅓% = .005⅓
$$= \frac{5\frac{1}{3}}{1000}$$
= 5⅓ ÷ 1000
= ¹⁶⁄₃ × ¹⁄₁₀₀₀
= ¹⁶⁄₃₀₀₀
= ²⁄₃₇₅
.5⅓% = ²⁄₃₇₅

7. Some fraction-percent equivalents are used so frequently that it is helpful to be familiar with them.

$\frac{1}{25} = 4\%$	$\frac{1}{5} = 20\%$
$\frac{1}{20} = 5\%$	$\frac{1}{4} = 25\%$
$\frac{1}{12} = 8\frac{1}{3}\%$	$\frac{1}{3} = 33\frac{1}{3}\%$
$\frac{1}{10} = 10\%$	$\frac{1}{2} = 50\%$
$\frac{1}{8} = 12\frac{1}{2}\%$	$\frac{2}{3} = 66\frac{2}{3}\%$
$\frac{1}{6} = 16\frac{2}{3}\%$	$\frac{3}{4} = 75\%$

Solving Percent Problems

8. Most percent problems involve three quantities:

- The rate, R, which is followed by a % sign
- The base, B, which follows the word "of"
- The amount or percentage, P, which usually follows the word "is"

a. If the rate (R) and the base (B) are known, then the percentage (P) = R × B.

Example: Find 15% of 50.
Solution: Rate = 15%
Base = 50
$$P = R \times B$$
$$P = 15\% \times 50$$
$$= .15 \times 50$$
$$= 7.5$$

15% of 50 is 7.5.

b. If the rate (R) and the percentage (P) are known, then the base (B) = $\frac{P}{R}$.

Example: 7% of what number is 35?
Solution: Rate = 7%
            Percentage = 35

$$B = \frac{P}{R}$$

$$B = \frac{35}{7\%}$$

$$= 35 \div .07$$

$$= 500$$

7% of 500 is 35.

c. If the percentage (P) and the base (B) are known, the rate $(R) = \frac{P}{B}$.

Example: There are 96 men in a group of 150 people. What percent of the group are men?
Solution: Base = 150
            Percentage (amount) = 96
                    Rate = $^{96}/_{150}$
                        = .64
                        = 64%

64% of the group are men.

Example: In a tank holding 20 gallons of solution, 1 gallon is alcohol. What is the strength of the solution in percent?
Solution: Percentage (amount) = 1 gallon
                    Base = 20 gallons
                    Rate = $^{1}/_{20}$
                        = .05
                        = 5%

The solution is 5% alcohol.

9. In a percent problem, the whole is 100%.

    Example: If a problem involves 10% of a quantity, the rest of the quantity is 90%.

    Example: If a quantity has been increased by 5%, the new amount is 105% of the original quantity.

    Example: If a quantity has been decreased by 15%, the new amount is 85% of the original quantity.

Shortcuts in Multiplication and Division

There are several shortcuts for simplifying multiplication and division. Following the description of each shortcut, practice problems are provided.

Dropping Final Zeros

1. a. A zero in a whole number is considered a "final zero" if it appears in the units column or if all columns to its right are filled with zeros. A final zero may be omitted in certain kinds of problems.

    b. In decimal numbers a zero appearing in the extreme right column may be dropped with no effect on the solution of a problem.

2. In multiplying whole numbers, the final zero(s) may be dropped during computation and simply transferred to the answer.

Examples:
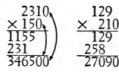

```
 2310            129          1760
× 150          × 210         × 205
─────          ─────        ─────
1155            129           880
 231            258           352
─────          ─────        ─────
346500         27090        360800
```

PRACTICE PROBLEMS

Solve the following multiplication problems, dropping the final zeros during computation.

1.	230 × 12	5.	430 × 360	8.	520 × 410
2.	175 × 130	6.	132 × 310	9.	634 × 120
3.	203 × 14	7.	350 × 24	10.	431 × 230
4.	621 × 140				

SOLUTIONS TO PRACTICE PROBLEMS

```
1.    230        3.    203        5.    430
    ×  12            ×  14            × 360
    ─────            ─────            ─────
      46              812             258
      23              203             129
    ─────            ─────            ─────
    2760             2842           154800
                  (no final zeros)
```

```
2.    175        4.    621        6.    132
    × 130            × 140            × 310
    ─────            ─────            ─────
     525             2484             132
     175              621             396
    ─────            ─────            ─────
   22750            86940           40920
```

7.
$$\begin{array}{r} 350 \\ \times\ 24 \\ \hline 140 \\ 70 \\ \hline 8400 \end{array}$$

9.
$$\begin{array}{r} 634 \\ \times\ 120 \\ \hline 1268 \\ 634 \\ \hline 76080 \end{array}$$

10.
$$\begin{array}{r} 431 \\ \times\ 230 \\ \hline 1293 \\ 862 \\ \hline 99130 \end{array}$$

8.
$$\begin{array}{r} 520 \\ \times\ 410 \\ \hline 52 \\ 208 \\ \hline 213200 \end{array}$$

Multiplying Whole Numbers by Decimals

3. In multiplying a whole number by a decimal number, if there are one or more final zeros in the multiplicand, move the decimal point in the multiplier to the right the same number of places as there are final zeros in the multiplicand. Then cross out the final zero(s) in the multiplicand.

Examples:
$$\begin{array}{r} 27500 \\ \times\ \ .15 \end{array} = \begin{array}{r} 275 \\ \times\ \ 15 \end{array}$$

$$\begin{array}{r} 1250 \\ \times\ .345 \end{array} = \begin{array}{r} 125 \\ \times\ 3.45 \end{array}$$

PRACTICE PROBLEMS

Rewrite the following problems, dropping the final zeros and moving decimal points the appropriate number of spaces. Then compute the answers.

1.
$$\begin{array}{r} 2400 \\ \times\ \ .02 \end{array}$$

2.
$$\begin{array}{r} 620 \\ \times\ \ .04 \end{array}$$

3.
$$\begin{array}{r} 800 \\ \times .005 \end{array}$$

4.	600 × .002	7.	400 × .04	9.	930 × .3
5.	340 × .08	8.	5300 × .5	10.	9000 × .001
6.	480 × .4				

SOLUTIONS TO PRACTICE PROBLEMS

The rewritten problems are shown, along with the answers.

1.	24 × 2 48	5.	34 × .8 27.2	8.	53 × 50 2650
2.	62 × .4 24.8	6.	48 × 4 192	9.	93 × 3 279
3.	8 × .5 4.0	7.	4 × 4 16	10.	9 × 1 9
4.	6 × .2 1.2				

Dividing by Whole Numbers

4. a. When there are final zeros in the divisor but no
    final zeros in the dividend, move the decimal

point in the dividend to the left as many places as there are final zeros in the divisor, then omit the final zeros.

Example: $2700.)\overline{37523.} = 27.)\overline{375.23}$

b. When there are fewer final zeros in the divisor than there are in the dividend, drop the same number of final zeros from the dividend as there are final zeros in the divisor.

Example: $250.)\overline{45300.} = 25.)\overline{4530.}$

c. When there are more final zeros in the divisor than there are in the dividend, move the decimal point in the dividend to the left as many places as there are final zeros in the divisor, then omit the final zeros.

Example: $2300.)\overline{690.} = 23.)\overline{6.9}$

d. When there are no final zeros in the divisor, no zeros can be dropped in the dividend.

Example: $23.)\overline{690.} = 23.)\overline{690.}$

PRACTICE PROBLEMS

Rewrite the following problems, dropping the final zeros and moving the decimal points the appropriate number of places. Then compute the quotients.

1. $600.)\overline{72.}$ 4. $46.)\overline{920.}$

2. $310.)\overline{6200.}$ 5. $11.0)\overline{220.}$

3. $7600)\overline{1520.}$ 6. $700.)\overline{84.}$

7. 90.)8100.

8. 8100.)1620.

9. 25.)5250.

10. 41.0)820.

11. 800.)96.

12. 650.)1300.

13. 5500.)110.

14. 36.)720.

15. 87.0)1740.

SOLUTIONS TO PRACTICE PROBLEMS

The rewritten problems are shown, along with the answers.

1.
```
      .12
6.).72
```

2.
```
      20
31.)620.
    62
    --
    00
```

3.
```
      .2
76.)15.2
    15 2
    ----
    0 0
```

4.
```
      20
46.)920.
    92
    --
    00
```

5.
```
       20
11.)220.
    22
    --
    00
```

6.
```
      .12
7.).84
```

7.
```
      90
9.)810.
```

8.
```
      .2
81.)16.2
    16 2
    ----
    0 0
```

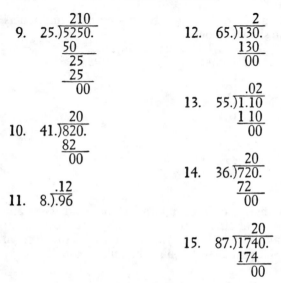

$$
\begin{array}{r}
210 \\
9.\ 25.)\overline{5250.} \\
50 \\
\hline
25 \\
25 \\
\hline
00
\end{array}
$$

$$
\begin{array}{r}
20 \\
10.\ 41.)\overline{820.} \\
82 \\
\hline
00
\end{array}
$$

$$
\begin{array}{r}
.12 \\
11.\ 8.)\overline{.96}
\end{array}
$$

$$
\begin{array}{r}
2 \\
12.\ 65.)\overline{130.} \\
130 \\
\hline
00
\end{array}
$$

$$
\begin{array}{r}
.02 \\
13.\ 55.)\overline{1.10} \\
1\ 10 \\
\hline
00
\end{array}
$$

$$
\begin{array}{r}
20 \\
14.\ 36.)\overline{720.} \\
72 \\
\hline
00
\end{array}
$$

$$
\begin{array}{r}
20 \\
15.\ 87.)\overline{1740.} \\
174 \\
\hline
00
\end{array}
$$

Division by Multiplication

5. Instead of dividing by a particular number, the same answer is obtained by multiplying by the equivalent multiplier.

6. To find the equivalent multiplier of a given divisor, divide 1 by the divisor.

   Example: The equivalent multiplier of 12½ is
   $$1 \div 12\frac{1}{2}$$
   or .08. The division problem 100 ÷ 12½ may be more easily solved as the multiplication problem 100 × .08. The answer will be the same.

7. Common divisors and their equivalent multipliers
   are shown below:

Divisor	Equivalent Multiplier
11⅑	.09
12½	.08
14²⁄₇	.07
16⅔	.06
20	.05
25	.04
33⅓	.03
50	.02

8. A divisor may be multiplied or divided by any
   power of 10, and the only change in its equivalent
   multiplier will be in the placement of the decimal
   point, as may be seen in the following table:

Divisor	Equivalent Multiplier
.025	40.
.25	4.
2.5	.4
25.	.04
250.	.004
2500.	.0004

PRACTICE PROBLEMS

Rewrite and solve each of the following problems by
using equivalent multipliers. Drop the final zeros where
appropriate.

1.	$100 \div 16\frac{2}{3} =$	11.	$955 \div 50 =$
2.	$200 \div 25 =$	12.	$300 \div 33\frac{1}{3} =$
3.	$300 \div 33\frac{1}{3} =$	13.	$275 \div 12\frac{1}{2} =$
4.	$250 \div 50 =$	14.	$625 \div 25 =$
5.	$80 \div 12\frac{1}{2} =$	15.	$244 \div 20 =$
6.	$800 \div 14\frac{2}{7} =$	16.	$350 \div 16\frac{2}{3} =$
7.	$620 \div 20 =$	17.	$400 \div 33\frac{1}{3} =$
8.	$500 \div 11\frac{1}{9} =$	18.	$375 \div 25 =$
9.	$420 \div 16\frac{2}{3} =$	19.	$460 \div 20 =$
10.	$1200 \div 33\frac{1}{3} =$	20.	$250 \div 12\frac{1}{2} =$

SOLUTIONS TO PRACTICE PROBLEMS

The rewritten problems are shown, along with the answers.

1. $100 \times .06 = 1 \times 6 = 6$
2. $200 \times .04 = 2 \times 4 = 8$
3. $300 \times .03 = 3 \times 3 = 9$
4. $250 \times .02 = 25 \times .2 = 5$
5. $80 \times .08 = 8 \times .8 = 6.4$
6. $800 \times .07 = 8 \times 7 = 56$
7. $620 \times .05 = 62 \times .5 = 31$

8. $500 \times .09 = 5 \times 9 = 45$

9. $420 \times .06 = 42 \times .6 = 25.2$

10. $1200 \times .03 = 12 \times 3 = 36$

11. $955 \times .02 = 19.1$

12. $300 \times .03 = 3 \times 3 = 9$

13. $275 \times .08 = 22$

14. $625 \times .04 = 25$

15. $244 \times .05 = 12.2$

16. $350 \times .06 = 35 \times .6 = 21$

17. $400 \times .03 = 4 \times 3 = 12$

18. $375 \times .04 = 15$

19. $460 \times .05 = 46 \times .5 = 23$

20. $250 \times .08 = 25 \times .8 = 20$

Multiplication by Division

9. Just as some division problems are made easier by changing them to equivalent multiplication problems, certain multiplication problems are made easier by changing them to equivalent division problems.

10. Instead of arriving at an answer by multiplying by a particular number, the same answer is obtained by dividing by the equivalent divisor.

11. To find the equivalent divisor of a given multiplier, divide 1 by the multiplier.

12. Common multipliers and their equivalent divisors are shown below:

Multiplier	Equivalent Divisor
11⅑	.09
12½	.08
14²⁄₇	.07
16⅔	.06
20	.05
25	.04
33⅓	.03
50	.02

Notice that the multiplier–equivalent divisor pairs are the same as the divisor–equivalent multiplier pairs given earlier.

PRACTICE PROBLEMS

Rewrite and solve each of the following problems by using division. Drop the final zeros where appropriate.

1. $77 \times 14²⁄₇ =$

2. $81 \times 11⅑ =$

3. $475 \times 20 =$

4. $42 \times 50 =$

5. $36 \times 33⅓ =$

6. $96 \times 12½ =$

7. $126 \times 16\frac{2}{3} =$ 14. $654 \times 16\frac{2}{3} =$

8. $48 \times 25 =$ 15. $154 \times 14\frac{2}{7} =$

9. $33 \times 33\frac{1}{3} =$ 16. $5250 \times 50 =$

10. $84 \times 14\frac{2}{7} =$ 17. $324 \times 25 =$

11. $99 \times 11\frac{1}{9} =$ 18. $625 \times 20 =$

12. $126 \times 33\frac{1}{3} =$ 19. $198 \times 11\frac{1}{9} =$

13. $168 \times 12\frac{1}{2} =$ 20. $224 \times 14\frac{2}{7} =$

SOLUTIONS TO PRACTICE PROBLEMS

The rewritten problems are shown, along with the answers.

1. $.07\overline{)77.} = 7\overline{)7700.}\,^{1100.}$ 6. $.08\overline{)96.} = 8\overline{)9600.}\,^{1200.}$

2. $.09\overline{)81.} = 9\overline{)8100.}\,^{900.}$ 7. $.06\overline{)126.} = 6\overline{)12600.}\,^{2100.}$

3. $.05\overline{)475.} = 5\overline{)47500.}\,^{9500.}$ 8. $.04\overline{)48.} = 4\overline{)4800.}\,^{1200.}$

4. $.02\overline{)42.} = 2\overline{)4200.}\,^{2100.}$ 9. $.03\overline{)33.} = 3\overline{)3300.}\,^{1100.}$

5. $.03\overline{)36.} = 3\overline{)3600.}\,^{1200.}$ 10. $.07\overline{)84.} = 7\overline{)8400.}\,^{1200.}$

11. $.09\overline{)99.} = 9\overline{)9900.}$ quotient $1100.$

16. $.02\overline{)5250.} = 2\overline{)525000.}$ quotient $262500.$

12. $.03\overline{)126.} = 3\overline{)12600.}$ quotient $4200.$

17. $.04\overline{)324.} = 4\overline{)32400.}$ quotient $8100.$

13. $.08\overline{)168.} = 8\overline{)16800.}$ quotient $2100.$

18. $.05\overline{)625.} = 5\overline{)62500.}$ quotient $12500.$

14. $.06\overline{)654.} = 6\overline{)65400.}$ quotient $10900.$

19. $.09\overline{)198.} = 9\overline{)19800.}$ quotient $2200.$

15. $.07\overline{)154.} = 7\overline{)15400.}$ quotient $2200.$

20. $.07\overline{)224.} = 7\overline{)22400.}$ quotient $3200.$

Powers and Roots

1. The numbers that are multiplied to give a product are called the **factors** of the product.

   Example: In $2 \times 3 = 6$, the numbers 2 and 3 are factors.

2. If the factors are the same, an **exponent** may be used to indicate the number of times the factor appears.

   Example: In $3 \times 3 = 3^2$, the number 3 appears as a factor twice, as is indicated by the exponent 2.

3. When a product is written in exponential form, the number the exponent refers to is called the **base**. The product itself is called the **power**.

Example: In 2^5, the number 2 is the base and 5 is the exponent.
$2^5 = 2 \times 2 \times 2 \times 2 \times 2 = 32$, so 32 is the power.

4.	a. If the exponent used is 2, we say that the base has been **squared**, or raised to the second power.

Example: 6^2 is read "six squared" or "six to the second power."

b. If the exponent used is 3, we say that the base has been **cubed**, or raised to the third power.

Example: 5^3 is read "five cubed" or "five to the third power."

c. If the exponent is 4, we say that the base has been raised to the fourth power. If the exponent is 5, we say the base has been raised to the fifth power, etc.

Example: 2^8 is read "two to the eighth power."

5.	A number that is the product of a number squared is called a **perfect square**.

Example: 25 is a perfect square because $25 = 5^2$.

6.	a. If a number has exactly two equal factors, each factor is called the **square root** of the number.

Example: $9 = 3 \times 3$; therefore, 3 is the square root of 9.

b. The symbol $\sqrt{}$ is used to indicate square root.

Example: $\sqrt{9} = 3$ means that the square root of 9 is 3, or $3 \times 3 = 9$.

7. The square root of the most common perfect squares may be found by using the following table, or by trial and error; that is, by finding the number that, when squared, yields the given perfect square.

Number	Perfect Square	Number	Perfect Square
1	1	10	100
2	4	11	121
3	9	12	144
4	16	13	169
5	25	14	196
6	36	15	225
7	49	20	400
8	64	25	625
9	81	30	900

Example: To find $\sqrt{81}$, note that 81 is the perfect square of 9, or $9^2 = 81$. Therefore, $\sqrt{81} = 9$.

8. To find the square root of a number that is not a perfect square, use the following method:
   a. Locate the decimal point.
   b. Mark off the digits in groups of two in both directions beginning at the decimal point.
   c. Mark the decimal point for the answer just above the decimal point of the number whose square root is to be taken.
   d. Find the largest perfect square contained in the left-hand group of two.
   e. Place its square root in the answer. Subtract the perfect square from the first digit or pair of digits.

f. Bring down the next pair.

g. Double the partial answer and add a trial digit to the right of the doubled partial answer. Multiply this new number by the trial digit. Place the correct new digit in the answer.

h. Subtract the product.

i. Repeat steps f–i as often as necessary.

You will notice that you get one digit in the answer for every group of two you marked off in the original number.

Example: Find the square root of 138,384.
Solution:

$$
\begin{array}{r}
3\ 7\ 2. \\
\sqrt{13'83'84.} \\
3^2 = \quad 9 \\
\hline
4\ 83 \\
7 \times 67 = \quad 4\ 69 \\
\hline
14\ 84 \\
2 \times 742 = \quad \underline{14\ 84}
\end{array}
$$

The number must first be marked off in groups of two figures each, beginning at the decimal point, which, in the case of a whole number, is at the right. The number of figures in the root will be the same as the number of groups so obtained.

The largest square less than 13 is 9. $\sqrt{9} = 3$

Place its square root in the answer. Subtract the perfect square from the first digit or pair of digits. Bring down the next pair. To form our trial divisor, annex 0 to this root "3" (making 30) and multiply by 2.

$483 \div 60 = 8$. Multiplying the trial divisor 68 by 8, we obtain 544, which is too large. We then try multiplying 67 by 7. This is correct. Add the trial digit to the right of the doubled partial answer. Place the new digit in the answer. Subtract the product. Bring down the final group. Annex 0 to the new root 37 and multiply by 2 for the trial divisor:

$$2 \times 370 = 740$$
$$1484 \div 740 = 2$$

Place the 2 in the answer.

The square root of 138,384 is 372.

Example: Find the square root of 3 to the nearest hundredth.

Solution:

$$
\begin{array}{r}
1.\ 7\ 3\ 2 \\
\sqrt{3.00'00'00}
\end{array}
$$

$1^2 =$	$\underline{1}$
20	2 00
$7 \times 27 =$	$\underline{1\ 89}$
340	11 00
$3 \times 343 =$	$\underline{10\ 29}$
3460	71 00
$2 \times 3462 =$	$\underline{69\ 24}$

The square root of 3 is 1.73 to the nearest hundredth.

9. To find the square root of a fraction, find the square root of its numerator and of its denominator.

Example: $\sqrt{4/9} = \dfrac{\sqrt{4}}{\sqrt{9}} = 2/3$

10.　a. If a number has exactly three equal factors, each factor is called the **cube root** of the number.

　　b. The symbol $\sqrt[3]{}$ is used to indicate the cube root.

Example:　$8 = 2 \times 2 \times 2$; therefore, $\sqrt[3]{8} = 2$

Order of Operations

Most formulas and other arithmetic problems involve more than one operation. There is a definite order which must be followed in evaluating formulas and other expressions:

a. Perform any operation within parentheses first.

b. Next, evaluate any powers and roots as they appear from left to right.

c. Next, perform all multiplications and divisions in order from left to right.

d. Finally, perform all additions and subtractions in order from left to right.

Example:　The formula for the perimeter of a rectangle is $P = 2l + 2w$. Find P if $l = 3$ and $w = 7$.

Solution:　　$P = 2l\ \ + 2w$

　　　　　　　$P = 2 \cdot 3 + 2 \cdot 7$

　　　　　　　$P = 6\ \ \ + 14$　　　Multiplication is done before addition.

　　　　　　　$P = 20$

Example: If Q = A − B(C − D), find Q when
A = 15, B = 2, C = 7 and D = 4.

Solution: Q = 15 − 2(7 − 4)
              Q = 15 − 2·3   The subtraction
                                      7 − 4 was in pa-
                                      rentheses and
                                      was therefore
                                      done first.
              Q = 15 − 6   The multiplica-
                                      tion is then
                                      done before the
                                      remaining sub-
              Q = 9   traction.

Example: If Y = M − N + 7, find Y when
M = 8 and N = 5.

Solution: Y = 8 − 5 + 7   Addition and
              Y = 3 + 7   subtraction are
              Y = 10   done in order
                                      from left to
                                      right.

Calculators

Many people use calculators to do basic arithmetic
with whole numbers and decimals. There are many different calculators available, some having percent keys,
square root keys, memories, various business functions,
trigonometric functions, and scientific functions. It is
best to learn to use your calculator by following the in-
struction manual that comes with it, or if that is not
available, by trying simple problems to which you know
the answers.

1. To use one very common kind of calculator, enter the numbers and operation symbols (+, −, ×, ÷) in the same order they might be written down in a problem. Call for the answer by pressing the "equals" (=) button.

   Example: Calculate 10 × 8.
   Solution: Press the buttons 10, ×, 8, and =, in that order. The answer 80 should appear in the display.

   Example: Calculate 8 + 3 − 4.
   Solution: Press the buttons 8, +, 3, −, 4, and =, in that order. The answer 7 should appear in the display.

2. Another common type of calculator does not have an "=" button but does have an "enter" button. To use this kind of calculator, the first number is pressed, then "enter," then the second number, then the operation button. The answer will then appear.

   Example: Calculate 7 − 4.
   Solution: Press 7, enter, 4, and −. The number 3 will appear on the display as your answer.

   Example: Calculate 18 ÷ 9.
   Solution: Press 18, enter, 9, and ÷. The answer 2 will appear.

3. To use a calculator for work with fractions, first convert the fraction to a decimal by dividing its numerator by its denominator.

Example: Calculate ⅞ × .6
Solution:
a. If your calculator has an "=" button, press 7, ÷, 8 (this converts ⅞ to the decimal .875, but it may not be shown on the display), ×, ., 6, and =. The answer .525 will be shown.

b. If your calculator has an "enter" button, press 7, enter, 8, ÷, enter, ., 6, ×. It may not be necessary to press "enter" the second time on your calculator. Try it to be sure.

4. To use a calculator for a problem containing several operations, follow the standard order of operations:

- Operations within parentheses first

- Powers and roots in order from left to right

- Multiplication and division in order from left to right

- Addition and subtraction in order from left to right

Example: Calculate $5 + 3(6 - 2)$.
Solution: $6 - 2$ must be found first, then the difference multiplied by 3, then this product added to 5.

a. If your calculator has an "=" button, press 6, −, 2, ×, 3, +, 5, and =. The answer 17 should appear.

b. If your calculator has an "enter" button, press 6, enter, 2, −, enter, 3, ×, enter, 5, +. The second and third "enter" may not be needed for your calculator.

MEASUREMENT
Tables of Measures

English Measures

Length

1 foot (ft or ′) = 12 inches (in or ″)
1 yard (yd) = 36 inches
1 yard = 3 feet
1 rod (rd) = 16½ feet
1 furlong = 40 rods
1 mile (mi) = 5280 feet
1 mile = 1760 yards
1 mile = 320 rods

Weight

1 pound (lb) = 16 ounces (oz)
1 hundredweight (cwt) = 100 pounds
1 ton (T) = 2000 pounds
1 long ton = 2240 pounds

Area

1 square foot (ft²) = 144 square inches (in²)
1 square yard (yd²) = 9 square feet

Liquid Measure

1 cup (c) = 8 fluid ounces (fl oz)
1 pint (pt) = 2 cups
1 pint = 4 gills (gi)
1 quart (qt) = 2 pints
1 gallon (gal) = 4 quarts
1 barrel (bl) = 31½ gallons

Dry Measure

1 quart (qt) = 2 pints (pt)
1 peck (pk) = 8 quarts
1 bushel (bu) = 4 pecks

Volume

1 cubic foot (ft³ or cu ft) = 1728 cubic inches
1 cubic yard (yd³ or cu yd) = 27 cubic feet
1 gallon = 231 cubic inches

58

General Measures

Time
1 minute (min) = 60 seconds (sec)
1 hour (hr) = 60 minutes
1 day = 24 hours
1 week = 7 days
1 year = 52 weeks
1 calendar year = 365 days

Angles and Arcs
1 minute (') = 60 seconds (")
1 degree (°) = 60 minutes
1 circle = 360 degrees

Paper Measure
1 quire = 24 sheets
1 ream = 20 quires
1 ream = 480 sheets
1 commercial ream = 500 sheets

Counting
1 dozen (doz) = 12 units
1 gross (gr) = 12 dozen
1 gross = 144 units
1 score = 20 units

Table of English–Metric Conversions (Approximate)

English to Metric
1 inch = 2.54 centimeters
1 yard = .9 meters
1 mile = 1.6 kilometers
1 ounce = 28 grams
1 pound = 454 grams
1 fluid ounce = 30 milliliters
1 liquid quart = .95 liters

Metric to English
1 centimeter = .39 inches
1 meter = 1.1 yards
1 kilometer = .6 miles
1 kilogram = 2.2 pounds
1 liter = 1.06 liquid quart

*Table of Metric Conversions**
1 liter = 1000 cubic centimeters (cm³)
1 milliliter = 1 cubic centimeter
1 liter of water weighs 1 kilogram
1 milliliter of water weighs 1 gram

The Metric System

——————————— LENGTH ———————————

Unit	Abbreviation	Number of Meters
myriameter	mym	10,000
kilometer	km	1,000
hectometer	hm	100
dekameter	dam	10
meter	m	1
decimeter	dm	0.1
centimeter	cm	0.01
millimeter	mm	0.001

——————————— AREA ———————————

Unit	Abbreviation	Number of Square Meters
square kilometer	sq km *or* km²	1,000,000
hectare	ha	10,000
are	a	100
centare	ca	1
square centi-meter	sq cm *or* cm²	0.0001

—————————————————————————————

* These conversions are exact only under specific conditions. If the conditions are not met, the conversions are approximate.

VOLUME

Unit	Abbreviation	Number of Cubic Meters
dekastere	das	10
stere	s	1
decistere	ds	0.10
cubic centimeter	cu cm or cm^3 or cc	0.000001

CAPACITY

Unit	Abbreviation	Number of Liters
kiloliter	kl	1,000
hectoliter	hl	100
dekaliter	dal	10
liter	l	1
deciliter	dl	0.10
centiliter	cl	0.01
milliliter	ml	0.001

MASS AND WEIGHT

Unit	Abbreviation	Number of Grams
metric ton	MT or t	1,000,000
quintal	q	100,000
kilogram	kg	1,000
hectogram	hg	100
dekagram	dag	10
gram	g or gm	1
decigram	dg	0.10
centigram	cg	0.01
milligram	mg	0.001

English and Metric Measurement

1. A **denominate number** is a number that specifies a given measurement. The unit of measure is called the **denomination**.

   Example: 7 miles, 3 quarts, and 5 grams are denominate numbers.

2. a. The English system of measurement uses such denominations as pints, ounces, pounds, and feet.

   b. The metric system of measurement uses such denominations as grams, liters, and meters.

English System of Measurement

3. To convert from one unit of measure to another, find in the Table of Measures how many units of the smaller denomination equal one unit of the larger denomination. This number is called the **conversion number**.

4. To convert from one unit of measure to a smaller unit, multiply the given number of units by the conversion number.

   Example: Convert 7 yards to inches.
   Solution:
   1 yard = 36 inches (conversion number)
   7 yards = 7 × 36 inches
   = 252 inches

Example: Convert 2 hours 12 minutes to minutes.
Solution:

$$1 \text{ hour} = 60 \text{ minutes (conversion number)}$$
$$2 \text{ hr } 12 \text{ min} = 2 \text{ hr} + 12 \text{ min}$$
$$2 \text{ hr} = 2 \times 60 \text{ min} = 120 \text{ min}$$
$$2 \text{ hr } 12 \text{ min} = 120 \text{ min} + 12 \text{ min}$$
$$= 132 \text{ min}$$

5. To convert from one unit of measure to a larger unit:

 a. Divide the given number of units by the conversion number.

Example: Convert 48 inches to feet.
Solution:

$$1 \text{ foot} = 12 \text{ inches (conversion number)}$$
$$48 \text{ in} \div 12 = 4 \text{ ft}$$

 b. If there is a remainder it is expressed in terms of the smaller unit of measure.

Example: Convert 35 ounces to pounds and ounces.
Solution:

$$1 \text{ pound} = 16 \text{ ounces (conversion number)}$$

$$35 \text{ oz} \div 16 = 16\overline{)35 \text{ oz}}^{\,2 \text{ lb}}$$
$$\frac{32}{3 \text{ oz}}$$
$$= 2 \text{ lb } 3 \text{ oz}$$

6. To add denominate numbers, arrange them in columns by common unit, then add each column. If necessary, simplify the answer, starting with the smallest unit.

Example: Add 1 yd 2 ft 8 in, 2 yd 2 ft 10 in, and 3 yd 1 ft 9 in.

Solution:

```
    1 yd 2 ft  8 in
    2 yd 2 ft 10 in
  + 3 yd 1 ft  9 in
  ─────────────────
    6 yd 5 ft 27 in
  = 6 yd 7 ft  3 in    (since 27 in = 2 ft 3 in)
  = 8 yd 1 ft  3 in    (since 7 ft = 2 yd 1 ft)
```

7. To subtract denominate numbers, arrange them in columns by common unit, then subtract each column starting with the smallest unit. If necessary, borrow to increase the number of a particular unit.

Example: Subtract 2 gal 3 qt from 7 gal 1 qt.

Solution:

```
    7 gal 1 qt =    6 gal 5 qt
  − 2 gal 3 qt = −  2 gal 3 qt
  ──────────────────────────
                   4 gal 2 qt
```

Note that 1 gal was borrowed from 7 gal.

$$1 \text{ gal} = 4 \text{ qt}$$

Therefore, 7 gal 1 qt = 6 gal 5 qt

8. To multiply a denominate number by a given number:

   a. If the denominate number contains only one unit, multiply the numbers and write the unit.

   Example: 3 oz × 4 = 12 oz

   b. If the denominate number contains more than one unit of measurement, multiply the number

of each unit by the given number and simplify
the answer, if necessary.

Example: Multiply 4 yd 2 ft 8 in by 2.
Solution:

$$
\begin{array}{r}
4 \text{ yd } 2 \text{ ft } \; 8 \text{ in} \\
\times \qquad\qquad 2 \\
\hline
8 \text{ yd } 4 \text{ ft } 16 \text{ in}
\end{array}
$$

= 8 yd 5 ft 4 in (since 16 in = 1 ft 4 in)
= 9 yd 2 ft 4 in (since 5 ft = 1 yd 2 ft)

9. To divide a denominate number by a given num-
    ber, convert all units to the smallest unit, then di-
    vide. Simplify the answer, if necessary.

Example: Divide 5 lb 12 oz by 4.
Solution: 1 lb = 16 oz, therefore
                 5 lb 12 oz = 92 oz
                 92 oz ÷ 4 = 23 oz
                           = 1 lb 7 oz

10. Alternate method of division:

   a. Divide the number of the largest unit by the
      given number.

   b. Convert any remainder to the next largest unit.

   c. Divide the total number of that unit by the
      given number.

   d. Again convert any remainder to the next unit
      and divide.

   e. Repeat until no units remain.

Example: Divide 9 hr 21 min 40 sec by 4.
Solution:

```
       2 hr     20 min      25 sec
   4)9 hr     21 min      40 sec
       8 hr
       1 hr = 60 min
               81 min
               80 min
                1 min =   60 sec
                         100 sec
                         100 sec
                           0 sec
```

Metric Measurement

11. The basic units of the metric system are the meter
     (m), which is used for length; the gram (g), which is
     used for weight; and the liter (*l*), which is used for
     capacity, or volume.

12. The prefixes that are used with the basic units, and
     their meanings, are:

Prefix	Abbreviation	Meaning
micro	μ	one millionth of (.000001)
milli	m	one thousandth of (.001)
centi	c	one hundredth of (.01)
deci	d	one tenth of (.1)
deka	da or dk	ten times (10)
hecto	h	one hundred times (100)
kilo	k	one thousand times (1000)
mega	M	one million times (1,000,000)

13. To convert *to* a basic metric unit from a prefixed metric unit, multiply by the number indicated in the prefix.

> *Example:* Convert 72 millimeters to meters.
> 72 millimeters = 72 × .001 meters
> = .072 meters

> *Example:* Convert 4 kiloliters to liters.
> 4 kiloliters = 4 × 1000 liters
> = 4000 liters

14. To convert *from* a basic unit to a prefixed unit, divide by the number indicated in the prefix.

> *Example:* Convert 300 liters to hectoliters.
> 300 liters = 300 ÷ 100 hectoliters
> = 3 hectoliters

> *Example:* Convert 4.5 meters to decimeters.
> 4.5 meters = 4.5 ÷ .1 decimeters
> = 45 decimeters

15. To convert from any prefixed metric unit to another prefixed unit, first convert to a basic unit, then convert the basic unit to the desired unit.

> *Example:* Convert 420 decigrams to kilograms.
> *Solution:* 420 dg = 420 × .1 g = 42 g
> 42 g = 42 ÷ 1000 kg = .042 kg

16. To add, subtract, multiply, or divide using metric measurement, first convert all units to the same unit, then perform the desired operation.

Example: Subtract 1200 g from 2.5 kg.
Solution:

$$\begin{array}{r} 2.5 \text{ kg} = 2500 \text{ g} \\ -\ 1200 \text{ g} = -1200 \text{ g} \\ \hline 1300 \text{ g} \end{array}$$

17. To convert from a metric measure to an English measure, or the reverse:

 a. In the Table of English–Metric Conversions (the table is on page 59), find how many units of the desired measure are equal to one unit of the given measure.

 b. Multiply the given number by the number found in the table.

Example: Find the number of pounds in 4 kilograms.
Solution: From the table, 1 kg = 2.2 lb.
4 kg = 4 × 2.2 lb
= 8.8 lb

Example: Find the number of meters in 5 yards.
Solution: 1 yd = .9 m
5 yd = 5 × .9 m
= 4.5 m

Temperature Measurement

1. The temperature measurement currently used in the United States is the degree Fahrenheit (°F). The

metric measurement for temperature is the degree Celsius (°C), also called degree Centigrade.

2. Degrees Celsius may be converted to degrees Fahrenheit by the formula:

$$°F = \tfrac{9}{5}°C + 32°$$

Example: Water boils at 100°C. Convert this to °F.

Solution:
$$°F = \tfrac{9}{5} \times \overset{20}{\cancel{100}} + 32°$$
$$= 180° + 32°$$
$$= 212°$$
$$100°C = 212°F$$

3. Degrees Fahrenheit may be converted to degrees Celsius by the formula:

$$°C = \tfrac{5}{9}(°F - 32°)$$

In using this formula, perform the subtraction in the parentheses first, then multiply by $\tfrac{5}{9}$.

Example: If normal body temperature is 98.6°F, what is it on the Celsius scale?
Solution:
$$°C = \tfrac{5}{9}(98.6° - 32°)$$
$$= \tfrac{5}{9} \times 66.6°$$
$$= \tfrac{333°}{9}$$
$$= 37°$$

Normal body temperature = 37°C.

Time

Types of Clocks

1. Time is usually measured using hours and minutes on a 12-hour clock. Anytime between midnight and noon is indicated by *a.m.*, and anytime between noon and midnight is indicated by *p.m.* Thus, 15 minutes after noon is 12:15 p.m., and 30 minutes after 4 in the morning is 4:30 a.m.

2. Military time is measured using a 24-hour clock, making the use of *a.m.* or *p.m.* unnecessary. The time is given as a four-digit number, where the left two digits indicate hours and the right two digits indicate minutes. Using this type of clock, midnight is 2400 hours, one minute past midnight is 0001, 3:40 a.m. is 0340, noon is 1200, and 3:40 p.m. is 1540. All a.m. times are between 0000 and 1200; all p.m. times are between 1200 and 2400.

Time Zones

3. Most of the United States falls within four time zones. From east to west, they are: Eastern Standard Time (EST), Central Standard Time (CST), Mountain Standard Time (MST), and Pacific Standard Time (PST). Each time zone is one hour earlier than the zone to its east.

    Example: At 2 p.m. EST, it is 1 p.m. CST, 12 noon MST, and 11 a.m. PST.

    Example: At 6 a.m. PST, it is 7 a.m. MST, 8 a.m. CST, and 9 a.m. EST.

Example: If a plane leaves Denver (Mountain Standard Time) at 3 p.m. and arrives in New York (Eastern Standard Time) 2 hours and 50 minutes later, it will arrive at 5:50 MST, which is 7:50 EST.

International Time Changes

4. The following table indicates the differences in time zones from the United States to other countries. The symbols are as follows:

> EST—Eastern Standard Time
> CST—Central Standard Time
> MST—Mountain Standard Time
> PST—Pacific Standard Time

Thus, if you wish to place a call, you are on Eastern Standard Time, and the chart indicates +3 under EST, it means that the country you wish to call is three hours later than your time. If the chart indicates −3 in the EST column, it means it is three hours earlier in the country you wish to call.

| | *Time Zone* | | | |
Country	EST	CST	MST	PST
American Samoa	−6	−5	−4	−3
Argentina	+2	+3	+4	+5
Australia	+16	+17	+18	+19
Austria	+6	+7	+8	+9
Belgium	+6	+7	+8	+9
Bolivia	+1	+2	+3	+4
Brazil	+2	+3	+4	+5

Country	Time Zone			
	EST	CST	MST	PST
Chile	+2	+3	+4	+5
Colombia	+0	+1	+2	+3
Costa Rica	−1	+0	+1	+2
Cyprus	+7	+8	+9	+10
Denmark	+6	+7	+8	+9
Equador	+0	+1	+2	+3
El Salvador	−1	+0	+1	+2
Fiji	+17	+18	+19	+20
Finland	+7	+8	+9	+10
France	+6	+7	+8	+9
Germany, Federal Republic of	+6	+7	+8	+9
Greece	+7	+8	+9	+10
Guam	+15	+16	+17	+18
Guatemala	−1	+0	+1	+2
Guyana	+2	+3	+4	+5
Haiti	+0	+1	+2	+3
Honduras	−1	+0	+1	+2
Hong Kong	+13	+14	+15	+16
Indonesia	+12	+13	+14	+15
Iran	+8½	+9½	+10½	+11½
Iraq	+8	+9	+10	+11
Ireland	+5	+6	+7	+8
Israel	+7	+8	+9	+10
Italy	+6	+7	+8	+9
Ivory Coast	+5	+6	+7	+8
Japan	+14	+15	+16	+17
Kenya	+8	+9	+10	+11

Country	Time Zone			
	EST	CST	MST	PST
Korea, Republic of	+14	+15	+16	+17
Kuwait	+8	+9	+10	+11
Liberia	+5	+6	+7	+8
Libya	+7	+8	+9	+10
Luxembourg	+6	+7	+8	+9
Malaysia	+12½	+13½	+14½	+15½
Monaco	+6	+7	+8	+9
Netherlands	+6	+7	+8	+9
New Zealand	+18	+19	+20	+21
Nicaragua	−1	+0	+1	+2
Nigeria	+6	+7	+8	+9
Norway	+6	+7	+8	+9
Panama	+0	+1	+2	+3
Paraguay	+2	+3	+4	+5
Peru	+0	+1	+2	+3
Philippines	+13	+14	+15	+16
Portugal	+5	+6	+7	+8
Rumania	+7	+8	+9	+10
Russia	+8	+9	+10	+11
Saudi Arabia	+8	+9	+10	+11
Senegal	+5	+6	+7	+8
Singapore	+12½	+13½	+14½	+15½
South Africa	+7	+8	+9	+10
Spain	+6	+7	+8	+9
Sri Lanka	10½	+11½	+12½	+13½
Sweden	+6	+7	+8	+9
Switzerland	+6	+7	+8	+9
Tahiti	−5	−4	−3	−2
Taiwan	+13	+14	+15	+16
Thailand	+12	+13	+14	+15
Tunisia	+6	+7	+8	+9
Turkey	+7	+8	+9	+10

	Time Zone			
Country	EST	CST	MST	PST
United Arab Emirates	+9	+10	+11	+12
United Kingdom	+5	+6	+7	+8
Vatican City	+6	+7	+8	+9
Venezuela	+1	+2	+3	+4
Yugoslavia	+6	+7	+8	+9

Calculating Number of Hours and Minutes

In many business situations, such as preparing payrolls, it is necessary to find the number of hours and minutes between two clock times.

5. If both times are in the period 1:00 a.m. to 12:59 p.m., or both are in the period 1:00 p.m. to 12:59 a.m., subtract the earlier time from the later time. Line the columns up carefully. If it is necessary to borrow from the hours column, remember to change the borrowed hour to 60 minutes.

    Example: What is the length of time between 7:30 a.m. and 12:45 p.m.?
    Solution: 12:45
                   − 7:30
                   ————
                     5:15   5 hours and 15 minutes

    Example: How much time has elapsed between 6:50 p.m. and 8:30 p.m.?

    Solution: 7 90
                   8:3̶0̶   Borrow 1 hour (60 min-
                   − 6:50   utes), then add 60 + 30
                   ————   = 90
                    1:40

The answer is 1 hour and 40 minutes.

6. If one of the times is in the period 1:00 a.m. to 12:59 p.m. and the other is in the period 1:00 p.m. to 12:59 a.m., add 12 hours to the later time, then subtract.

Example: Find the length of time from 9:15 a.m. to 3:45 p.m.
Solution: 3:45 + 12:00 = 15:45

```
   15:45
 −  9:15
   ─────
   6:30
```

The answer is 6 hours and 30 minutes.

Calculating Number of Months and Days

7. One method of finding the number of months and days from one date to the next is by counting them as they appear on the calendar. This gives the exact number of days.

Example: To find the number of days from March 10 to April 20, add the remaining 21 days in March to 20 days in April, for 41 days.

Example: To find the number of days from July 5 to September 5, add the 26 remaining days in July to 31 days in August, then add 5 days in September, for 62 days.

8. A second method is often used in business situations. The year is considered to have 360 days, which is 12 months of 30 days each. With this method, each

month is as long as every other month. To find the number of months and days from one date to another, subtract, borrowing 1 month (30 days) when necessary.

Example: Find the number of days from August 15 to October 10:

Month	*Day*	
9	40	
~~10~~	~~10~~	Borrow 1 month, then
− 8	15	add 30 days to 10 days.
1	25	

1 month and 25 days, or 55 days

9. When the 360-day year is used, it is convenient to represent any number of days as a fractional part of the year:

$$1 \text{ day } = \text{ }^{1}/_{360} \text{ year}$$
$$30 \text{ days} = \text{ }^{30}/_{360} \text{ year} = \text{ }^{1}/_{12} \text{ year}$$
$$60 \text{ days} = \text{ }^{60}/_{360} \text{ year} = \text{ }^{1}/_{6} \text{ year}$$
$$90 \text{ days} = \text{ }^{90}/_{360} \text{ year} = \text{ }^{1}/_{4} \text{ year}$$

Geometry

Angles

1. Angles are measured using *degrees* (°). **Right** angles have 90°, **straight** angles have 180°, **acute** angles have between 0° and 90°, and **obtuse** angles have between 90° and 180°.

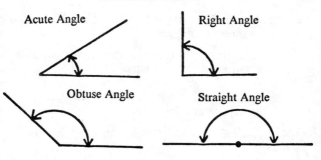

Acute Angle

Right Angle

Obtuse Angle

Straight Angle

Triangles

2. A triangle is a closed, three-sided figure. The figures below are all triangles.

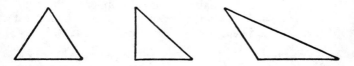

   a. The sum of the three angles of a triangle is 180°.

   b. To find an angle of a triangle when you are given the other two angles, add the given angles and subtract their sum from 180°.

Example: Two angles of a triangle are 60° and 40°. Find the third angle.
Solution: 60° + 40° = 100°
          180° − 100° = 80°

          The third angle is 80°.

3. a. A triangle that has two equal sides is called an **isosceles triangle**.

   b. In an isosceles triangle, the angles opposite the equal sides are also equal.

4. a. A triangle that has all three sides equal is called an **equilateral triangle**.

   b. Each angle of an equilateral triangle is 60°.

5. a. A triangle that has a right angle is called a **right triangle**.

   b. In a right triangle, the sum of the two acute angles is 90°.

   c. In a right triangle, the side opposite the right angle is called the **hypotenuse** and is the longest side. The other two sides are called **legs**.

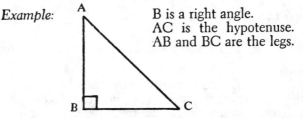

Example: B is a right angle.
AC is the hypotenuse.
AB and BC are the legs.

6. The **Pythagorean theorem** states that in a right triangle, the square of the hypotenuse equals the sum of the squares of the legs.

7. To find the hypotenuse of a right triangle when given the legs:

a. Square each leg.

b. Add the squares.

c. Find the square root of this sum.

Example: In a right triangle the legs are 6 inches and 8 inches. Find the hypotenuse.

Solution: $6^2 = 36$ $8^2 = 64$
$36 + 64 = 100$
$\sqrt{100} = 10$

The hypotenuse is 10 inches.

8. To find a leg when given the other leg and the hypotenuse of a right triangle:

a. Square the hypotenuse and the given leg.

b. Subtract the square of the leg from the square of the hypotenuse.

c. Find the square root of this difference.

Example: One leg of a right triangle is 12 feet and the hypotenuse is 20 feet. Find the other leg.

Solution: $12^2 = 144$ $20^2 = 400$
$400 - 144 = 256$
$\sqrt{256} = 16$

The other leg is 16 feet.

Quadrilaterals

9. a. A **quadrilateral** is a closed, four-sided figure in two dimensions. Common quadrilaterals are the **parallelogram, rectangle,** and **square.**

    b. The sum of the four angles of a quadrilateral is 360°.

10. **a.** A **parallelogram** is a quadrilateral in which both pairs of opposite sides are parallel (∥).

    b. Opposite sides of a parallelogram are also equal.

    c. Opposite angles of a parallelogram are equal.

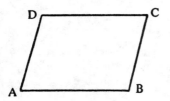

In parallelogram ABCD,
AB ∥ CD, AD ∥ BC
AB = CD, AD = BC
angle A = angle C,
angle B = angle D

11. A **rectangle** has all of the properties of a parallelogram. In addition, all four of its angles are right angles.

12. A **square** is a rectangle having the additional property that all four of its sides are equal.

Circles

13. A **circle** is a closed plane curve, all points of which are equidistant from a point within called the **center**.

14. A line segment from any point on the circle to the center is called a **radius**. A **diameter** is a line segment which passes through the center and connects two points on the circle. The diameter of a circle is equal to twice its radius.

15. a. A complete circle contains 360°.

    b. A semicircle contains 180°.

Perimeter

16. The **perimeter** of a two-dimensional figure is the distance around the figure.

Example: The perimeter of the figure above is $9 +$
$8 + 4 + 5 + 3 = 29$.

17.   a. The perimeter of a triangle is found by adding
all of its sides.

Example: If the sides of a triangle are 4, 5, and 7,
its perimeter is $4 + 5 + 7 = 16$.

   b. If the perimeter and two sides of a triangle are
given, the third side is found by adding the two
given sides and subtracting this sum from the
perimeter.

Example: Two sides of a triangle are 12 and 15,
and the perimeter is 37. Find the other side.
Solution: $12 + 15 = 27$
        $37 - 27 = 10$

   The third side is 10.

18.   The perimeter of a rectangle equals twice the sum
of the length and the width. The formula is
        $P = 2(l + w)$.

Example: The perimeter of a rectangle whose
length is 7 feet and width is 3 feet equals $2 \times 10 =$
20 feet.

19. The perimeter of a square equals one side multiplied by 4. The formula is P = 4s.

   Example: The perimeter of a square, one side of which is 5 feet, is 4 × 5 feet = 20 feet.

20. a. The circumference of a circle is the distance around the circle.

   b. The circumference of a circle is equal to the product of the diameter multiplied by π. The formula is C = πd.

   c. The number π ("pi") is approximately equal to $^{22}\!/_{7}$, or 3.14 (3.1416 for greater accuracy). A problem will usually state which value to use; otherwise, express the answer in terms of "pi," π.

   Example: The circumference of a circle whose diameter is 4 inches = 4π inches; or, if it is stated that $\pi = {^{22}\!/_{7}}$, then the circumference is $4 \times {^{22}\!/_{7}} = {^{88}\!/_{7}} = 12\frac{4}{7}$ inches.

   d. Since the diameter is twice the radius, the circumference equals twice the radius multiplied by π. The formula is C = 2πr.

   Example: If the radius of a circle is 3 inches, then the circumference = 6π inches.

   e. The diameter of a circle equals the circumference divided by π.

   Example: If the circumference of a circle is 11 inches, then, assuming

$$\pi = {}^{22}\!/_7,$$

diameter = $11 \div {}^{22}\!/_7$ inches

$$= 11 \times \overset{1}{\cancel{7}}\!/_{\underset{2}{\cancel{22}}} \text{ inches}$$

$$= {}^7\!/_2 \text{ inches, or } 3\tfrac{1}{2} \text{ inches}$$

Area

21. **a.** In a figure of two dimensions, the total space within the figure is called the **area**.

   b. Area is expressed in square denominations, such as square inches, square centimeters, and square miles.

   c. In computing area, all dimensions must be expressed in the same denomination.

22. The area of a square is equal to the square of the length of any side. The formula is $A = s^2$.

   Example: The area of a square, one side of which is 6 inches, is $6 \times 6 = 36$ square inches.

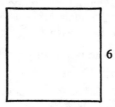

23. **a.** The area of a rectangle equals the product of the length multiplied by the width. The length is

any side; the width is the side next to the length. The formula is A = *l* × *w*.

Example: If the length of a rectangle is 6 feet and its width 4 feet, then the area is 6 × 4 = 24 square feet.

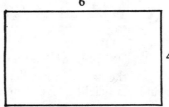

b. If given the area of a rectangle and one dimension, divide the area by the given dimension to find the other dimension.

Example: If the area of a rectangle is 48 square feet and one dimension is 4 feet, then the other dimension is 48 ÷ 4 = 12 feet.

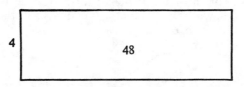

24. a. The altitude, or height, of a parallelogram is a line drawn from a vertex perpendicular to the opposite side, or base.

Example: DE is the height. AB is the base.

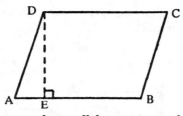

b. The area of a parallelogram is equal to the product of its base and its height: $A = b \times h$.

Example: If the base of a parallelogram is 10 centimeters and its height is 5 centimeters, its area is $5 \times 10 = 50$ square centimeters.

c. If given one of these dimensions and the area, divide the area by the given dimension to find the base or the height of a parallelogram.

Example: If the area of a parallelogram is 40 square inches and its height is 8 inches, its base is $40 \div 8 = 5$ inches.

25. a. The altitude, or height, of a triangle is a line drawn from a vertex perpendicular to the opposite side, called the base.

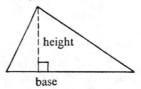

b. The area of a triangle is equal to one-half the product of the base and the height: $A = \frac{1}{2}b \times h$.

Example: The area of a triangle having a height of
5 inches and a base of 4 inches is
  ½ × 4 × 5 = ½ × 20 = 10 square inches.

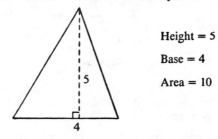

Height = 5

Base = 4

Area = 10

c. In a right triangle, one leg may be considered
the height and the other leg the base. Therefore,
the area of a right triangle is equal to one-half
the product of the legs.

Example: The legs of a right triangle are 3 and 4.
Its area is ½ × 3 × 4 = 6 square units.

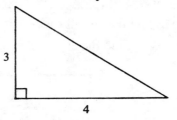

26.   a. The area of a circle is equal to the radius
squared, multiplied by π: $A = \pi r^2$.

Example: If the radius of a circle is 6 inches, then
the area = 36π square inches.

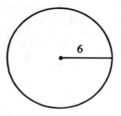

b. To find the radius of a circle given the area, divide the area by π and find the square root of the quotient.

Example: To find the radius of a circle of area 100π:

$$\frac{100\pi}{\pi} = 100$$
$$\sqrt{100} = 10 = \text{radius}$$

27. Some figures are composed of several geometric shapes. To find the area of such a figure it is necessary to find the area of each of its parts.

Example: Find the area of the figure below:

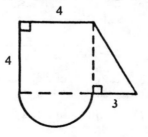

Solution: The figure is composed of three parts: **a square** of side 4, a semicircle of diameter 4 (the lower side of the square), and a right triangle with legs 3 and 4 (the right side of the square).

$$\text{Area of square} = 4^2 = 16$$
$$\text{Area of triangle} = \tfrac{1}{2} \times 3 \times 4 = 6$$

Area of semicircle is ½ area of circle $= \tfrac{1}{2}\pi r^2$

$$\text{Radius} = \tfrac{1}{2} \times 4 = 2$$
$$\text{Area} = \tfrac{1}{2}\pi r^2$$
$$= \tfrac{1}{2} \times \pi \times 2^2$$
$$= 2\pi$$

Total area $= 16 + 6 + 2\pi = 22 + 2\pi$.

Three-Dimensional Figures

28. a. In a three-dimensional figure, the total space contained within the figure is called the **volume**; it is expressed in **cubic denominations**.

    b. The total outside surface is called the **surface area**; it is expressed in **square denominations**.

    c. In computing volume and surface area, all dimensions must be expressed in the same denomination.

29. a. A **rectangular solid** is a figure of three dimensions having six rectangular faces meeting each other at right angles. The three dimensions are length, width and height.

    The figure below is a rectangular solid; *l* is the length, *w* is the width, and *h* is the height.

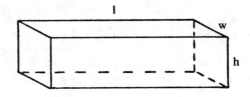

b. The volume of a rectangular solid is the product of the length, width, and height:
$$V = l \times w \times h.$$

Example: The volume of a rectangular solid whose length is 6 feet, width 3 feet, and height 4 feet is $6 \times 3 \times 4 = 72$ cubic feet.

30. a. A **cube** is a rectangular solid whose edges are equal. The figure below is a cube; the length, width, and height are all equal to *e*.

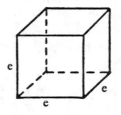

   b. The volume of a cube is equal to the edge
      cubed: $V = e^3$.

Example: The volume of a cube whose height is 6
inches equals $6^3 = 6 \times 6 \times 6 = 216$ cubic inches.

   c. The surface area of a cube is equal to the area of
      any side multiplied by 6.

Example: The surface area of a cube whose length
is 5 inches $= 5^2 \times 6 = 25 \times 6 = 150$ square inches.

31.   The volume of a **circular cylinder** is equal to the
     product of π, the radius squared, and the height.

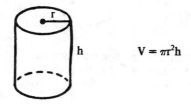

$$V = \pi r^2 h$$

Example: A circular cylinder has a radius of 7
inches and a height of ½ inch. Using $\pi = \frac{22}{7}$, its volume is $\frac{22}{7} \times 7 \times 7 \times \frac{1}{2} = 77$ cubic inches.

32   The volume of a **sphere** is equal to ⅓ the product of
     π and the radius cubed.

$$V = \frac{4}{3}\pi r^3$$

Example: If the radius of a sphere is 3 cm, its volume in terms of π is:

⅓ × π × 3 cm × 3 cm × 3 cm = 36π cm³

33. The volume of a cone is given by the formula
$$V = ⅓\pi r^2 h,$$
where *r* is the radius and *h* is the height.

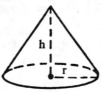

Example: In the cone shown, if h = 9 cm, r = 10 cm, and π = 3.14, then the volume is:
⅓ × 3.14 × 10 × 10 × 9 cm³ = 3.14 × 300 *cm³*
= 942 cm³

34. The volume of a **pyramid** is given by the formula V = ⅓Bh, where *B* is the area of the base and *h* is the height.

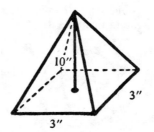

Example: In the pyramid shown, the height is 10″ and the side of the base is 3″. Since the base is a square, B = 3² = 9 square inches.

V = ⅓ × 9 × 10 = 30 cubic inches

Latitude and Longitude

1. Imaginary lines that circle the earth and are parallel to the equator are called *parallels of latitude.* The equator is considered 0°. A parallel north of the equator is denoted by N and a parallel south of the equator is denoted by S. The North Pole is 90° N and the South Pole is 90° S.

   Examples: New York City is at about 40° N, or 40 degrees north of the equator. Rio de Janeiro, Brazil, is at about 23° S; this is 23 degrees south of the equator.

2. Imaginary lines on the earth's surface that pass through the North Pole and the South Pole are circles called *meridians of longitude.* The Prime Meridian, which passes through Greenwich, England, is considered 0°; the meridian called the International Date Line is 180°. Meridians to the west of Greenwich, from 0° to 180°, are called west longitude (W). Meridians to the east of Greenwich, from 0° to 180°, are called *east longitude* (E).

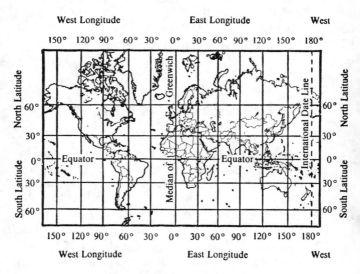

Map of the World

Examples: Los Angeles is at approximately 120°
W. It is 120 degrees west of the Prime Meridian.
Helsinki, in Finland, is at approximately 25° E, or
25 degrees east of the Prime Meridian.

3. a. For greater accuracy, both latitude and longitude
        are usually given using degrees and minutes (').
        There are 60 minutes in each degree.

    Example: 32° 15' W is between 32° and 33° west
    longitude.

b. For even greater accuracy, seconds ('') may be used. There are 60 seconds in 1 minute.

4. Any point on the earth can be located if its latitude and longitude are known.

Example: Sydney, Australia, is located at 33° 55' S, 151° 10' E. This means that it is almost 34° south of the equator and about 151° east of Greenwich, England.

Example: Dallas, Texas, is located at 32° 47' N, 96° 48' W. This is 32° 47' north of the equator and 96° 48' west of Greenwich, England.

Transportation

Distance

1. In distance problems, there are usually three quantities involved: the distance (in miles), the rate (in miles per hour—mph), and the time (in hours).

a. To find the distance, multiply the rate by the time.

Example: A man traveling 40 miles an hour for 3 hours travels 40×3 or 120 miles.

b. The rate is the distance traveled in unit time. To find the rate, divide the distance by the time.

Example: If a car travels 100 miles in 4 hours, the rate is $100 \div 4$ or 25 miles an hour.

c. To find the time, divide the distance by the rate.

Example: If a car travels 150 miles at the rate of 30 miles an hour, the time is 150 ÷ 30 or 5 hours.

2. a. When two people or objects are traveling towards each other, the rate at which they are approaching each other is the sum of their respective rates.

   b. When two people or objects are traveling in directly opposite directions, the rate at which they are separating is the sum of their respective rates.

3. To solve problems involving combined rates:

   a. Determine which of the three factors is to be found.
   b. Combine the rates and find the unknown factor.

Example: A and B are walking towards each other over a road 120 miles long. A walks at a rate of 6 miles an hour, and B walks at a rate of 4 miles an hour. How soon will they meet?
Solution: The factor to be found is the time.

$$\text{Time} = \text{distance} \div \text{rate}$$
$$\text{Distance} = 120 \text{ miles}$$
$$\text{Rate} = 6 + 4 = 10 \text{ miles an hour}$$
$$\text{Time} = 120 \div 10 = 12 \text{ hours}$$

They will meet in 12 hours.

Example: Joe and Sam are walking in opposite directions. Joe walks at the rate of 5 miles an hour, and Sam walks at the rate of 7 miles an hour. How far apart will they be at the end of 3 hours?

Solution: The factor to be found is distance.
Distance = time × rate
Time = 3 hours
Rate = 5 + 7 = 12 miles an hour
Distance = 12 × 3 = 36 miles

They will be 36 miles apart at the end of 3 hours.

4. To find the time it takes a faster person or object to catch up with a slower person or object:

a. Determine how far ahead the slower person or object is.

b. Subtract the slower rate from the faster rate to find the gain in rate per unit time.

c. Divide the distance that has been gained by the difference in rates.

Example: Two automobiles are traveling along the same road. The first one, which travels at the rate of 30 miles an hour, starts out 6 hours ahead of the second one, which travels at the rate of 50 miles an hour. How long will it take the second auto to catch up with the first one?
Solution: The first automobile starts out 6 hours ahead of the second. Its rate is 30 miles an hour. Therefore, it has traveled 6 × 30 or 180 miles by the time the second one starts. The second automobile travels at the rate of 50 miles an hour. Therefore, its gain is 50 − 30 or 20 miles an hour. The second auto has to cover 180 miles. Therefore, it will take 180 ÷ 20 or 9 hours to catch up with the first automobile.

5. In some problems, two or more rates must be averaged. When the times are the same for two or more different rates, add the rates and divide by the number of rates.

Example: If a man travels for 2 hours at 30 miles an hour, at 40 miles an hour for the next 2 hours, and at 50 miles an hour for the next 2 hours, then his average rate for the 6 hours is $(30 + 40 + 50) \div 3 = 40$ miles an hour.

6. When the times are not the same, but the distances are the same:

   a. Assume the distance to be a convenient length.

   b. Find the time at the first rate.

   c. Find the time at the second rate.

   d. Find the time at the third rate, if any.

   e. Add up all the distances and divide by the total time to find the average rate.

Example: A boy travels a certain distance at the rate of 20 miles an hour and returns at the rate of 30 miles an hour. What is his average rate for both trips?
Solution: The distance is the same for both trips. Assume that it is 60 miles. The time for the first trip is $60 \div 20 = 3$ hours. The time for the second trip is $60 \div 30 = 2$ hours. The total distance is 120 miles. The total time is 5 hours. The average rate for both trips is

$$120 \div 5 = 24 \text{ miles an hour.}$$

7. When the times are not the same and the distances are not the same:

   a. Find the time for the first distance.

   b. Find the time for the second distance.

   c. Find the time for the third distance, if any.

   d. Add up all the distances and divide by the total time to find the average rate.

   Example: A man travels 100 miles at 20 miles an hour, 60 miles at 30 miles an hour, and 80 miles at 10 miles an hour. What is his average rate for the three trips?
   Solution: The time for the first trip is $100 \div 20 = 5$ hours. The time for the second trip is $60 \div 30 = 2$ hours. The time for the third trip is $80 \div 10 = 8$ hours. The total distance is 240 miles. The total time is 15 hours. Average rate is $240 \div 15 = 16$ miles an hour.

Fuel

8. Problems involving miles per gallon (mpg) of gasoline are solved in the same way as those involving miles per hour. The word "gallon" simply replaces the word "hour."

9. Miles per gallon = distance in miles ÷ no. of gallons.

   Example: If a car can travel 100 miles using 4 gallons of gasoline, then its gasoline consumption is $100 \div 4$, or 25 mpg.

BUSINESS STATISTICS

Graphs

1. Graphs illustrate comparisons and trends in statistical information. The most commonly used graphs are bar graphs, line graphs, circle graphs, and pictographs.

Bar Graphs

2. Bar graphs are used to compare various quantities. Each bar may represent a single quantity or may be divided to represent several quantities.

3. Bar graphs may have horizontal or vertical bars.

   The questions below refer to graph on page 101.

   Question 1:   What was the approximate municipal expenditure per capita in cities having populations of 200,000 to 299,000?
   Answer: The middle bar of the seven shown represents cities having populations from 200,000 to 299,000. This bar reaches about halfway between 100 and 200. Therefore, the per capita expenditure was approximately $150.

   Question 2:   Which cities spent the most per capita on health, education, and welfare?
   Answer: The bar for cities having populations of 1,000,000 and over has a larger striped section than

Municipal Expenditures, Per Capita

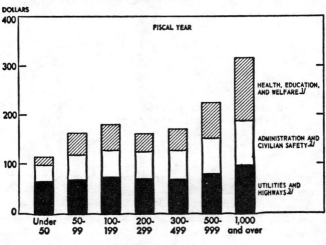

DOLLARS

FISCAL YEAR

HEALTH, EDUCATION, AND WELFARE.[1]

ADMINISTRATION AND CIVILIAN SAFETY.[2]

UTILITIES AND HIGHWAYS.[3]

CITY POPULATION (THOUSANDS)

[1] PUBLIC WELFARE, EDUCATION, HOSPITALS, HEALTH, LIBRARIES, AND HOUSING AND URBAN RENEWAL
[2] POLICE AND FIRE PROTECTION, FINANCIAL ADMINISTRATION, GENERAL CONTROL, GENERAL PUBLIC BUILDINGS, INTEREST ON GENERAL DEBT, AND OTHER.
[3] HIGHWAYS, SEWERAGE, SANITATION, PARKS AND RECREATION, AND UTILITIES.

the other bars. Therefore, those cities spent the most.

Question 3: Of the three categories of expenditures, which was least dependent on city size?
Answer: The expenditures for utilities and highways, the darkest part of each bar, varied least as city size increased.

Line Graphs

4. Line graphs are used to show trends, often over a period of time.

5. A line graph may include more than one line, with each line representing a different item.

    Illustration:
    The graph below indicates at 5-year intervals the number of citations issued for various offenses from the year 1960 to the year 1980.

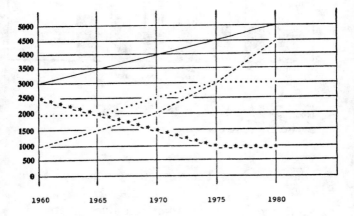

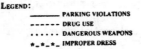

LEGEND:
————— PARKING VIOLATIONS
- - - - - DRUG USE
• • • • • • DANGEROUS WEAPONS
*_*_*_ IMPROPER DRESS

Question 4:   Over the 20-year period, which offense shows an average rate of increase of more than 150 citations per year?
Answer: Drug use citations increased from 1000 in 1960 to 4500 in 1980. The average increase over the 20-year period is $3500/20 = 175$.

Question 5:   Over the 20-year period, which offense shows a constant rate of increase or decrease?
Answer: A straight line indicates a constant rate of increase or decrease. Of the four lines, the one representing parking violations is the only straight one.

Question 6:   Which offense shows a total increase or decrease of 50% for the full 20-year period?
Answer: Dangerous weapons citations increased from 2000 in 1960 to 3000 in 1980, which is an increase of 50%.

Circle Graphs

6.   Circle graphs are used to show the relationship of various parts of a quantity to each other and to the whole quantity.

7.   Percents are often used in circle graphs. The 360 degrees of the circle represents 100%.

8.   Each part of the circle graph is called a **sector**.

Illustration:
The following circle graph shows how the federal budget of $300.4 billion was spent.

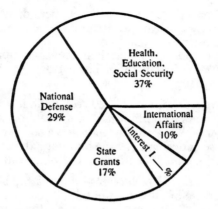

Question 7: What is the value of I?
Answer: There must be a total of 100% in a circle graph. The sum of the other sectors is:

$$17\% + 29\% + 37\% + 10\% = 93\%$$

Therefore, I = 100% − 93% = 7%.

Question 8: How much money was actually spent on national defense?
Answer:
   29% × $300.4 billion = $87.116 billion
                        = $87,116,000,000

Question 9: How much more money was spent on state grants than on interest?
Answer:
   17% − 7% = 10%
   10% × $300.4 billion = $30.04 billion
                        = $30,040,000,000

Pictographs

9. Pictographs allow comparisons of quantities by using symbols. Each symbol represents a given number of a particular item.

Illustration:

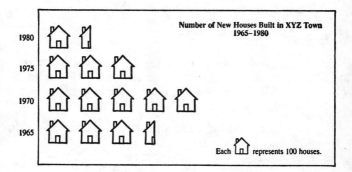

Question 10: How many more new houses were built in 1970 than in 1975?
Answer: There are two more symbols for 1970 than for 1975. Each symbol represents 100 houses. Therefore, 200 more houses were built in 1970.

Question 11: How many new houses were built in 1965?
Answer: There are 3½ symbols shown for 1965; 3½ × 100 = 350 houses.

Question 12: In which year were half as many houses built as in 1975?

Answer: In 1975, $3 \times 100 = 300$ houses were built. Half of 300, or 150, houses were built in 1980.

Statistics

1. The averages used in statistics include the **arithmetic mean**, the **median**, and the **mode**.

Mean

2. a. The most commonly used average of a group of numbers is the arithmetic mean. It is found by adding the numbers given and then dividing this sum by the number of items being averaged.

    Example: Find the arithmetic mean of 2, 8, 5, 9, 6, and 12.
    Solution: There are 6 numbers.

    $$\text{Arithmetic mean} = \frac{2 + 8 + 5 + 9 + 6 + 12}{6}$$
    $$= \frac{42}{6}$$
    $$= 7$$

    The arithmetic mean is 7.

    b. If a problem calls for simply the "average" or the "mean," it is referring to the arithmetic mean.

Median

3. If a group of numbers is arranged in order, the middle number is called the median. If there is no single

middle number (this occurs when there is an even number of items), the median is found by computing the arithmetic mean of the two middle numbers.

Example: The median of 6, 8, 10, 12, and 14 is 10.

Example: The median of 6, 8, 10, 12, 14, and 16 is the arithmetic mean of 10 and 12:

$$\frac{10 + 12}{2} = \frac{22}{2} = 11$$

Mode

4. The mode of a group of numbers is the number that appears most often.

    Example: The mode of 10, 5, 7, 9, 12, 5, 10, 5, and 9 is 5.

Weighted Averages

5. To obtain the average of quantities that are weighted:

    a. Set up a table listing the quantities, their respective weights, and their respective values.

    b. Multiply the value of each quantity by its respective weight.

    c. Add up these products.

    d. Add up the weights.

    c. Divide the sum of the products by the sum of the weights.

Example: In a particular company, two employees received hourly wages of $4.50, three employees received hourly wages of $4.15, and five employees received hourly wages of $4.75. Find the average hourly wage of this group of employees.

Solution:

Hourly Wage	Weight	Product
$4.50	2	$ 9.00
4.15	3	12.45
4.75	5	23.75
Total	10	$45.20

$45.20 ÷ 10 = $4.52
The average hourly wage is $4.52

Probability

1. The study of probability deals with predicting the outcome of chance events—that is, events in which one has no control over the results.

   Example: Tossing a coin, rolling dice, and drawing concealed objects from a bag are chance events.

2. The probability of a particular outcome is equal to the number of ways that outcome can occur, divided by the total number of possible outcomes.

   Example: In tossing a coin, there are 2 possible outcomes: heads or tails. The probability that the coin will turn up heads is $1 ÷ 2$ or ½.

   Example: If a bag contains 5 balls of which 3 are red, the probability of drawing a red ball is ⅗. The probability of drawing a non-red ball is ⅖.

3. a. If an event is certain, its probability is 1.

    Example: If a bag contains only red balls, the probability of drawing a red ball is 1.

    b. If an event is impossible, its probability is 0.

    Example: If a bag contains only red balls, the probability of drawing a green ball is 0.

4. Probability may be expressed in fractional, decimal, or percent form.

    Example: An event having a probability of ½ is said to be 50% probable.

5. A probability determined by random sampling of a group of items is assumed to apply to other items in that group and in other similar groups.

    Example: A random sampling of 100 items produced in a factory shows that 7 are defective. How many items of the total production of 50,000 can be expected to be defective?
    Solution: The probability of an item being defective is 7/100, or 7%. Of the total production, 7% can be expected to be defective.

    $$7\% \times 50,000 = .07 \times 50,000 = 3500$$

    3500 items can be expected to be defective.

BUSINESS APPLICATIONS

Payroll

Salaries

1. **Salaries** are computed over various time periods: hourly, daily, weekly, biweekly (every 2 weeks), semi-monthly (twice each month), monthly, and yearly.

2. **Overtime** is usually computed as "time and a half"; that is, each hour in excess of the number of hours in the standard workday or workweek is paid at $1\frac{1}{2}$ times the regular hourly rate. Some companies pay "double time," twice the regular hourly rate, for work on Sundays and holidays.

    Example: An employee is paid weekly, based on a 40-hour workweek, with time and a half for overtime. If the employee's regular hourly rate is $4.50, how much will he earn for working 47 hours in one week?
    Solution:
        Overtime hours = 47 − 40 = 7 hours
          Overtime pay = $1\frac{1}{2}$ × $4.50 = $6.75 per hour
    Overtime pay for 7 hours:
          7 × $6.75 = $47.25
    Regular pay for 40 hours:
          40 × $4.50 = $180.00
              Total pay = $47.25 + $180 = $227.25

Time Sheets

3. Payroll may be computed from time sheets similar to the one on the following page.

    Example: On 1/6–1/7, Adams worked his regular 8-hour shift from 11:00 p.m. until 7:00 a.m. He then worked an overtime assignment of 2½ hours, from 7:00 a.m. until 9:30 a.m. As the table shows, his regular hourly rate is $5.76 and his overtime rate is $8.64 (which is 1½ × $5.76).

Regular pay: 8 × $5.76 = $46.08

Overtime pay: 2½ × $8.64 = $\frac{5}{2} \times \overset{4.32}{\underset{1}{\$8.64}}$ = $21.60

Total pay: $46.08 + 21.60 = $67.68

Example: Dana worked a regular 8-hour shift from 7:00 a.m. until 3:00 p.m. at $4.80 per hour. The overtime assignment was 1 hour 20 minutes, or 1⅓ hours, at $7.20 per hour.

Regular pay: 8 × $4.80 = $38.40

Overtime pay: 1⅓ × $7.20 = $\frac{1}{3} \times \overset{2.40}{\underset{1}{\$7.20}}$ = $9.60

Total pay: $38.40 + 9.60 = $48.00

Commissions

4. a. In occupations such as retail sales, real estate, and insurance, earnings may be based on **commission**, which is a percent of the sales or a percent of the value of the transactions that are completed.

EMPLOYEES' TIME SHEET

Pay No.	Name	Hourly Rate	Time Reporting				Time Leaving		Time Actually worked		Pay due
			Date	A.M.	P.M.	Date	A.M.	P.M.	Hrs.	Mins.	
REGULAR ASSIGNMENT											
27	Adams	$ 5.76	1-6-93		11:00	1-7-93	7:00		8	00	46.08
35	Beers	4.25	1-7-93		3:00	1-7-93		11:00	8	00	34.00
98	Coyne	7.50	1-7-93	7:00		1-7-93		3:00	8	00	60.00
72	Dana	4.80	1-7-93	7:00		1-7-93		3:00	8	00	38.40
56	Ellis	5.20	1-7-93		3:00	1-7-93		11:00	8	00	41.60
87	Flint	7.20	1-8-93	7:00		1-8-93		3:00	8	00	57.60
39	Grew	4.25	1-8-93		3:00	1-8-93		11:00	8	00	34.00
41	Hare	6.00	1-9-93		3:00	1-9-93		11:00	8	00	48.00
14	James	5.90	1-10-93		11:00	1-11-93	7:00		8	00	47.20
OVERTIME ASSIGNMENT											
27	Adams	8.64	1-7-93	7:00		1-7-93	9:30		2	30	21.60
35	Beers	6.38	1-7-93		11:00	1-7-93		11:20	0	20	2.13
98	Coyne	11.25	1-7-93		3:00	1-7-93		4:20	1	20	15.00
72	Dana	7.20	1-7-93		3:00	1-7-93		4:20	1	20	9.60
56	Ellis	7.80	1-7-93		11:00	1-7-93		11:40	0	40	5.20
87	Flint	10.80	1-8-93		3:00	1-8-93		4:00	1	00	10.80
39	Grew	6.38	1-8-93		11:00	1-8-93		11:50	0	50	5.32
41	Hare	9.00	1-9-93		11:00	1-10-93	12:30		1	30	13.50
14	James	8.85	1-11-93	7:00		1-11-93	8:00		1	00	8.85

b. Earnings may be from straight commission only, from salary plus commission, or from a commission that is graduated according to transaction volume.

Example: A salesman earns a salary of $200 weekly, plus a commission based on sales volume for the week. The commission is 7% for the first $1500 of sales and 10% for all sales in excess of $1500. How much did he earn in a week in which his sales totaled $3200?

Solution:

$3200 − $1500 = $1700 excess sales
  .07 × $1500 = $105 commission on first $1500
  .10 × $1700 = $170 commission on excess sales
               + $200 weekly salary
                 $475 total earnings

5. Gross pay refers to the amount of money earned whether from salary, commission, or both, before any deductions are made.

Payroll Deductions

6. There are several deductions that are usually made from gross pay:

a. Withholding tax is the amount of money withheld for income tax. It is based on wages, marital status, and number of exemptions (also called allowances) claimed by the employee. The current withholding tax is found by referring to tables supplied by the federal, state or city governments.

Example:

Married Persons—Weekly Payroll Period

Wages		Number of withholding allowances claimed				
At least	But less than	0	1	2	3	4
		Amount of income tax to be withheld				
400	410	73.00	67.60	62.30	57.70	53.10
410	420	75.80	70.40	65.00	60.10	55.50
420	430	78.60	73.20	67.80	62.50	57.90
430	440	81.40	76.00	70.60	65.20	60.30
440	450	84.20	78.80	73.40	68.00	62.70
450	460	87.00	81.60	76.20	70.80	65.40
460	470	90.20	84.40	79.00	73.60	68.20
470	480	93.40	87.30	81.80	76.40	71.00
480	490	96.60	90.50	84.60	79.20	73.80
490	500	99.80	93.70	87.50	82.00	76.60

Based on the above table, an employee who is married, claims three exemptions, and is paid a weekly wage of $434.50 will have $65.20 withheld for income tax. If the same employee earned $440 weekly it would be necessary to look on the next line for "at least $440 but less than $450" to find that $68.00 would be withheld.

b. The FICA (Federal Insurance Contribution Act) tax is also called the Social Security tax. In a recent year the FICA tax was 6.2% on wages up to $55,500 annual wages; wages in excess of $55,500 were not subject to the tax.

The FICA that year was found by multiplying wages by .062 or by using a table such as that on page 115. Using the table, the FICA on wages of $379 is $23.50. ($6.20 for each $100 times 3 = $18.60 plus $4.90 for the $79 comes to $23.50.)

Example:

Employee Social Security (6.2%) Tax Deduction Table.

If wage payment is—	The employee tax to be deducted is—	If wage payment is—	The employee tax to be deducted is—
68.00	4.22	**88.00**	5.46
69.00	4.28	**89.00**	5.52
70.00	4.34	**90.00**	5.58
71.00	4.40	**91.00**	5.64
72.00	4.46	**92.00**	5.70
73.00	4.53	**93.00**	5.77
74.00	4.59	**94.00**	5.83
75.00	4.65	**95.00**	5.89
76.00	4.71	**96.00**	5.95
77.00	4.77	**97.00**	6.01
78.00	4.84	**98.00**	6.08
79.00	4.90	**99.00**	6.14
80.00	4.96	**100.00**	6.20

c. The Employee Medicare Tax deduction that same year was 1.45% on wages up to $130,200. The payroll deduction is computed in the same way as the FICA deduction, using Medicare figures.

d. Other deductions that may be made from gross pay are deductions for pension plans, loan payments, payroll savings plans, and union dues.

The **net pay,** or **take-home pay,** is equal to gross pay less the total deductions.

Example: Mr. Jay earns $550 salary per week, with the following deductions: federal withholding tax,

$106.70; FICA tax, $34.10; Medicare tax $7.98; state tax, $22.83; pension payment, $6.42; union dues, $5.84. How much take-home pay does he receive?

Solution:　Deductions:　　　　$106.70
　　　　　　　　　　　　　　　　34.10
　　　　　　　　　　　　　　　　 7.98
　　　　　　　　　　　　　　　　22.83
　　　　　　　　　　　　　　　　 6.42
　　　　　　　　　　　　　　　　 5.84
　　　　　　　　　　　　　　　$183.87

Gross pay　　=　　$550.00
Deductions　 =　 − 183.87
Net pay　　　=　　$366.13

His take-home pay is $366.13

Profit and Loss

1. The following terms may be encountered in profit and loss problems:

   a. The **cost price** of an article is the price paid by a person who wishes to sell it again.

   b. There may be an **allowance** or **trade discount** on the cost price.

   c. The **list price** or **marked price** is the price at which the article is listed or marked to be sold.

   d. There may be a **discount** or series of discounts on the list price.

   e. The **selling price** or **sales price** is the price at which the article is finally sold.

f. If the selling price is greater than the cost price, there has been a profit.

g. If the selling price is lower than the cost price, there has been a loss.

h. If the article is sold at the same price as the cost, there has been no loss or profit.

i. Profit or loss may be based either on the cost price or on the selling price.

j. Profit or loss may be stated in terms of dollars and cents, or in terms of percent.

k. **Overhead** expenses include such items as rent, salaries, etc., and may be added to cost price or to the profit to increase the selling price.

2. The basic formulas used in profit and loss problems are:

> Selling price = cost price + profit
> Selling price = cost price − loss

Example: If the cost of an article is \$2.50, and the profit is \$1.50, then the selling price is \$2.50 + \$1.50 = \$4.00.

Example: If the cost of an article is \$3.00, and the loss is \$1.20, then the selling price is \$3.00 − \$1.20 = \$1.80.

3. a. To find the profit in terms of money, subtract the cost price from the selling price, or

> selling price − cost price = profit.

Example: If an article costing $3.00 is sold for $5.00, the profit is $5.00 − $3.00 = $2.00.

b. To find the loss in terms of money, subtract the selling price from the cost price, or
cost price − selling price = loss.

Example: If an article costing $2.00 is sold for $1.50, the loss is $2.00 − $1.50 = $.50.

4. To find the selling price if the profit or loss is expressed in percent based on cost price:

a. Multiply the cost price by the percent of profit or loss to find the profit or loss in terms of money.

b. Add this product to the cost price if a profit is involved, or subtract for a loss.

Example: Find the selling price of an article costing $3.00 that was sold at a profit of 15% of the cost price.
Solution: 15% of $3.00 = .15 × $3.00
                              = $.45 profit
             $3.00 + $.45 = $3.45

Selling price = $3.45

Example: If an article costing $2.00 is sold at a loss of 5% of the cost price, find the selling price.
Solution: 5% of $2.00 = .05 × $2.00
                             = $.10 loss
             $2.00 − $.10 = $1.90

Selling price = $1.90

5. To find the cost price when given the selling price and the percent of profit or loss based on the selling price:

   a. Multiply the selling price by the percent of profit or loss to find the profit or loss in terms of money.

   b. Subtract this product from the selling price if profit, or add the product to the selling price if a loss.

   Example: If an article sells for $12.00 and there has been a profit of 10% of the selling price, what is the cost price?
   Solution: 10% of $12.00 = .10 × $12.00
                                    = $1.20 profit
   $12.00 − $1.20 = $10.80

   Cost price = $10.80

   Example: What is the cost price of an article selling for $2.00 on which there has been a loss of 6% of the selling price?
   Solution: 6% of $2.00 = .06 × $2.00
                                 = $.12 loss
   $2.00 + $.12 = $2.12

   Cost price = $2.12

6. To find the percent of profit or percent of loss based on cost price:

   a. Find the profit or loss in terms of money.

   b. Divide the profit or loss by the cost price.

   c. Convert to a percent.

Example: Find the percent of profit based on cost price of an article costing $2.50 and selling for $3.00.

Solution: $3.00 − $2.50 = $.50 profit

$$2.50\overline{).50} = 250\overline{)50.00} \quad \overset{.20}{}$$
$$.20 = 20\%$$

Profit = 20%

Example: Find the percent of loss based on cost price of an article costing $5.00 and selling for $4.80.

Solution: $5.00 − $4.80 = $.20 loss

$$5.00\overline{).20} = 500\overline{)20.00} \quad \overset{.04}{}$$
$$.04 = 4\%$$

Loss = 4%

7. To find the percent of profit or percent of loss on selling price:

   a. Find the profit or loss in terms of money.

   b. Divide the profit or loss by the selling price.

   c. Convert to a percent.

Example: Find the percent of profit based on the selling price of an article costing $2.50 and selling for $3.00.

Solution: $3.00 − $2.50 = $.50 profit

$$3.00\overline{).50} = 300\overline{)50.00} = .16\tfrac{2}{3}$$
$$= 16\tfrac{2}{3}\%$$

Profit = 16⅔%

Example: Find the percent of loss based on the selling price of an article costing $5.00 and selling for $4.80.

Solution: $5.00 − $4.80 = $.20 loss

$$4.80\overline{)\,.20\,} = 480\overline{)20.00} = .04\tfrac{1}{6}$$
$$= 4\tfrac{1}{6}\%$$

Loss = $4\tfrac{1}{6}\%$

8. To find the cost price when given the selling price and the percent of profit based on the cost price:

   a. Establish a relation between the selling price and the cost price.

   b. Solve to find the cost price.

   Example: An article is sold for $2.50, which is a 25% profit of the cost price. What is the cost price?
   Solution: Since the selling price represents the whole cost price plus 25% of the cost price,

   $$2.50 = 125\% \text{ of the cost price}$$
   $$2.50 = 1.25 \text{ of the cost price}$$
   $$\text{Cost price} = 2.50 \div 1.25$$
   $$= 2.00$$

   Cost price = $2.00

9. To find the selling price when given the profit based on the selling price:

   a. Establish a relation between the selling price and the cost price.

   b. Solve to find the selling price.

Example: A merchant buys an article for $27.00 and sells it at a profit of 10% of the selling price. What is the selling price?

Solution: $27.00 + profit = selling price

Since the profit is 10% of the selling price, the cost price must be 90% of the selling price.

$$27.00 = 90\% \text{ of the selling price}$$
$$= .90 \text{ of the selling price}$$
$$\text{Selling price} = 27.00 \div .90$$
$$= 30.00$$

Selling price = $30.00

Trade Discounts

Single Discounts

1. A trade discount, usually expressed in percent, indicates a part that is to be deducted from the list price.

2. To find the selling price when given the list price and the trade discount:

   a. Multiply the list price by the percent of discount to find the discount in terms of money.

   b. Subtract the discount from the list price.

   Example: The list price of an article is $20.00. There is a discount of 5%. What is the selling price?

Solution:

$20.00 × 5% = 20.00 × .05 = $1.00 discount

$20.00 − $1.00 = $19.00

Selling price = $19.00

3. An alternate method of solving the above problem is to consider the list price to be 100%. Then, if the discount is 5%, the selling price is 100% − 5% = 95% of the list price. The selling price is

95% of $20.00 = .95 × $20.00
= $19.00

Series of Discounts

4. There may be more than one discount to be deducted from the list price. These are called a **discount** series.

To find the selling price when given the list price and a discount series:

a. Multiply the list price by the first percent of discount.

b. Subtract this product from the list price.

c. Multiply the difference by the second discount.

d. Subtract this product from the difference.

e. Continue the same procedure if there are more discounts.

Example: Find the selling price of an article listed at $10.00 on which there are discounts of 20% and 10%.

Solution:
$$\$10.00 \times 20\% = 10.00 \times .20 = \$2.00$$
$$\$10.00 - \$2.00 = \$8.00$$
$$\$8.00 \times 10\% = 8.00 \times .10 = \$.80$$
$$\$8.00 - \$.80 = \$7.20$$

Selling price = $7.20

5. Instead of deducting each discount individually, it is often more practical to find the single equivalent discount first and then deduct. It does not matter in which order the discounts are taken.

6. The single equivalent discount may be found by assuming a list price of 100%. Leave all discounts in percent form.

   a. Subtract the first discount from 100%, giving the net cost factor (NCF) had there been only one discount.

   b. Multiply the NCF by the second discount. Subtract the product from the NCF, giving a second NCF that reflects both discounts.

   c. If there is a third discount, multiply the second NCF by it and subtract the product from the second NCF, giving a third NCF that reflects all three discounts.

   d. If there are more discounts, repeat the process of multiplying and subtracting.

   e. Subtract the final NCF from 100% to find the single equivalent discount.

Example: Find the single equivalent discount of 20%, 25%, and 10%.
Solution:

$$
\begin{array}{rl}
& 100\% \\
- & \underline{20\%} \quad \text{first discount} \\
& 80\% \quad \text{first NCF} \\
-25\% \text{ of } 80\% = & \underline{20\%} \\
& 60\% \quad \text{second NCF} \\
-10\% \text{ of } 60\% = & \underline{6\%} \\
& 54\% \quad \text{third NCF}
\end{array}
$$

100% − 54% = 46% single equivalent discount

Example: An article lists at $750.00. With discounts of 20%, 25%, and 10%, what is the selling price of this article?
Solution: As shown above, the single equivalent discount of 20%, 25%, and 10% is 46%.

$$
\begin{aligned}
46\% \text{ of } \$750 &= .46 \times \$750 \\
&= \$345 \\
\$750 - \$345 &= \$405 \\
\text{Selling price} &= \$405
\end{aligned}
$$

Invoices

1. An invoice is a bill for the sale of goods. It includes the name of the seller, the name of the buyer, the date of sale, the terms of sale, the type and quantity of the goods sold, and the price of the goods. The example on the following page is a typical invoice.

E Z Rite Office Supplies, Inc.
123 Any Street
Bigtown, N.J. 00004

Date <u>MAY 15, 19—</u>

To: HOME REALTY CO., INC.
505 N. 6th Street
SOMETOWN, N.H. 26734

Terms: N/30

Quantity	Description	Unit Price	Amount
3 REAMS	TYPING PAPER	$ 8.25	$ 24.75
5 DOZ.	MEMO PADS	5.00	25.00
6	DESK CALENDARS	4.50	27.00
			$ 76.75

Terms

2. The terms on the invoice are the conditions of sale. They indicate when the payment is due and if there are discounts for payment before the due date.

Examples:

n/30	net amount due in 30 days
n/e.o.m.	net amount due at the end of the month
n/10 e.o.m.	net amount due 10 days after the end of the month
n/10 r.o.g.	net amount due 10 days after receipt of the goods
c.o.d.	cash on delivery
2/10, n/30	2% discount if payment made in 10 days; otherwise payment due in 30 days

| 2/15, 1/30, n/60 | 2% discount if payment is made in 15 days, or 1% discount if payment is made from 16th day to 30th day; else pay full amount by 60th day from date of invoice. |

Due Date

3. a. If the terms on an invoice are given in days, find the due date by counting days from the date of the invoice.

   Example: An invoice dated May 15, with terms n/30, has a due date 30 days from May 15; the due date is June 14.

   b. If the terms are given in months, the due date is found by counting calendar months from the date of the invoice.

   Example: An invoice dated February 20 is due in two months. Its due date is April 20.

Calculating Amount Due

4. A discount indicated in the terms of the invoice must be considered in calculating the actual amount due.

   Example: An invoice dated April 15 for $152.83 has terms 1/10, n/30. If payment is made in 10 days (by April 25), 1% of $152.83 must be deducted:

$$\begin{array}{r} \$152.83 \\ -\ \ 1.53 \\ \hline \$151.30 \end{array}$$

less 1% of 152.83

Alternately, the amount may be found by computing 99% of $152.83.

The amount due by April 25 is $151.30. If payment is not made by April 25, then the full amount is due by May 15.

Interest

1. Interest (I) is the price paid for the use of money. There are three items considered in interest:

   a. The **principal** (p), which is the amount of money bearing interest.

   b. The **interest rate** (r), expressed in percent on an annual basis.

   c. The **time** (t) during which the principal is used, expressed in terms of a year.

2. The basic formulas used in interest problems are:

   a. $I = prt$

   b. $p = \dfrac{I}{rt}$

   c. $r = \dfrac{I}{pt}$

   d. $t = \dfrac{I}{pr}$

3. a. For most interest problems, the year is considered to have 360 days. Months are considered to have 30 days, unless a particular month is specified.

    b. To use the interest formulas, time must be expressed as part of a year.

    Examples: 5 months = $\frac{5}{12}$ year
                36 days = $\frac{36}{360}$ year, or $\frac{1}{10}$ year
                1 year 3 months = $\frac{15}{12}$ year, or $\frac{5}{4}$ year

    c. In reference to time, the prefix *semi* means "every half." The prefix *bi* means "every two."

    Examples: *Semiannually* means every half-year (every 6 months).
                Biannually means every 2 years.
                Semimonthly means every half-month (every 15 days, unless the month is specified).
                Biweekly means every 2 weeks (every 14 days).

4. There are two types of interest problems:

    a. Simple interest, in which the interest is calculated only once over a given period of time.

    b. Compound interest, in which interest is recalculated at given time periods based on previously earned interest.

Simple Interest

5. To find the interest when the principal, rate, and time are given:

a. Change the rate of interest to a fraction.

b. Express the time as a fractional part of a year.

c. Multiply all three items.

Example: Find the interest on $400 at 11¼% for 3 months and 16 days.

Solution: $11\frac{1}{4}\% = \frac{45}{4}\% = \frac{45}{400}$

   3 months and 16 days = 106 days
       (30 days per month)

   106 days = $\frac{106}{360}$ of a year = $\frac{53}{180}$ year
       (360 days per year)

$$\overset{1}{400} \times \frac{45}{400} \times \frac{53}{180} = \frac{53}{4}$$

$$= 13.25$$

Interest = $13.25

6. To find the principal if the interest, interest rate, and time are given:

a. Change the interest rate to a fraction.

b. Express the time as a fractional part of a year.

c. Multiply the rate by the time.

d. Divide the interest by this product.

Example: What amount of money invested at 6% would receive interest of $18 over 1½ years?

Solution: $6\% = \frac{6}{100}$

   $1\frac{1}{2}$ years = $\frac{3}{2}$ years

$$\overset{3}{\frac{6}{100}} \times \frac{3}{2} = \frac{9}{100}$$

$$\$18 \div \%_{100} = \$\overset{2}{\cancel{18}} \times \overset{}{100}\cancel{\%}_1$$
$$= \$200$$

Principal $= \$200$

7. To find the rate if the principal, time, and interest are given:

   a. Change the time to a fractional part of a year.

   b. Multiply the principal by the time.

   c. Divide the interest by this product.

   d. Convert to a percent.

   Example: At what interest rate should $300 be invested for 40 days to accrue $2 in interest?

   Solution: 40 days $= {}^{40}\!/_{360}$ of a year

   $$\overset{5}{\cancel{300}} \times \overset{20}{\cancel{{}^{40}\!/_{360}}}_{\underset{3}{\cancel{6}}} = 100/3$$

   $$\$2 \div 100/3 = \overset{1}{\cancel{2}} \times {}^{3}\!/_{\underset{50}{\cancel{100}}}$$
   $$= {}^{3}\!/_{50}$$
   $${}^{3}\!/_{50} = 6\%$$

   Interest rate $= 6\%$

8. To find the time (in years) if the principal, interest, and interest rate are given:

   a. Change the interest rate to a fraction (or decimal).

   b. Multiply the principal by the rate.

c. Divide the interest by this product.

Example: Find the length of time for which $240 must be invested at 5% to accrue $16 in interest.

Solution: 5% = .05
      240 × .05 = 12
      16 ÷ 12 = 1⅓

Time = 1⅓ years

Compound Interest

9. Interest may be computed on a compound basis; that is, the interest at the end of a certain period (half year, full year, or whatever time stipulated) is added to the principal for the next period. The interest is then computed on the new increased principal, and for the next period the interest is again computed on the new increased principal. Since the principal constantly increases, compound interest yields more than simple interest.

10. To find the compound interest when given the principal, rate, and time period:

a. Calculate the interest as for simple interest problems, using the period of compounding for the time.

b. Add the interest to the principal.

c. Calculate the interest on the new principal over the period of compounding.

d. Add this interest to form a new principal.

e. Continue the same procedure until all periods required have been accounted for.

f. Subtract the original principal from the final principal to find the compound interest.

Example: Find the amount that $200 will become if compounded semiannually at 8% for 1½ years.
Solution: Since it is to be compounded semiannually for 1½ years, the interest will have to be computed 3 times:

Interest for
the first
period: $.08 \times \frac{1}{2} \times \$200 = \$8$

First new
principal: $\$200 + \$8 = \$208$

Interest for
the second
period: $.08 \times \frac{1}{2} \times \$208 = \$8.32$

Second new
principal: $\$208 + \$8.32 = \$216.32$

Interest for
the third
period: $.08 \times \frac{1}{2} \times \$216.32 = \$8.6528$

Final
principal: $\$216.32 + \$8.6528 = \$224.9728$

Answer: $224.97 to the nearest cent

Bank Discounts

11. A promissory note is a commitment to pay a certain amount of money on a given date, called the **date of maturity**.

12. When a promissory note is cashed by a bank in advance of its date of maturity, the bank deducts a discount from the principal and pays the rest to the depositor.

13. To find the bank discount:

   a. Find the time between the date the note is deposited and its date of maturity, and express this time as a fractional part of a year.

   b. Change the rate to a fraction.

   c. Multiply the principal by the time and the rate to find the bank discount.

   d. If required, subtract the bank discount from the original principal to find the amount the bank will pay the depositor.

Example: A $400 note drawn up on August 12, 19--, for 90 days is deposited at the bank on September 17, 19--. The bank charges a 6½% discount on notes. How much will the depositor receive?

Solution: From August 12, 19--, to September 17, 19--, is 36 days. This means that the note has 54 days to run.

$$54 \text{ days} = {}^{54}\!/_{360} \text{ of a year}$$
$$6\tfrac{1}{2}\% = 13\tfrac{1}{2}\% = {}^{13}\!/_{200}$$
$$\$400 \times {}^{13}\!/_{200} \times {}^{54}\!/_{360} = {}^{39}\!/_{10}$$
$$= \$3.90$$
$$\$400 - \$3.90 = \$396.10$$

The depositor will receive $396.10.

Taxation

1. The following facts should be taken into consideration when computing taxation problems:

   a. Taxes may be expressed as a percent or in terms of money based on a certain denomination.

   b. A **surtax** is an additional tax besides the regular tax rate.

2. In taxation, there are usually three items involved: the amount taxable, henceforth called the **base**, the tax rate, and the tax itself.

3. To find the tax when given the base and the tax rate in percent:

   a. Change the tax rate to a decimal.

   b. Multiply the base by the tax rate.

   Example: How much would be realized on $4000 if taxed 15%?
   Solution: $15\% = .15$
   $$\$4000 \times .15 = \$600$$

   $$\text{Tax} = \$600$$

4. To find the tax rate in percent form when given the base and the tax:

   a. Divide the tax by the base.

   b. Convert to a percent.

   Example: Find the tax rate at which $5600 would yield $784.

Solution: $\$784 \div \$5600 = .14$
$.14 = 14\%$

Tax rate = 14%

5. To find the base when given the tax rate and the tax:

   a. Change the tax rate to a decimal.

   b. Divide the tax by the tax rate.

   Example: What amount of money taxed 3% would yield $75?
   Solution: $3\% = .03$
   $\$75 \div .03 = \$2500$

   Base = $2500

6. When the tax rate is fixed and expressed in terms of money, take into consideration the denomination upon which it is based; that is, whether it is based on every $100, or $1000, etc.

7. To find the tax when given the base and the tax rate in terms of money:

   a. Divide the base by the denomination upon which the tax rate is based.

   b. Multiply this quotient by the tax rate.

   Example: If the tax rate is $3.60 per $1000, find the tax on $470,500.
   Solution: $\$470,500 \div \$1000 = 470.5$
   $470.5 \times \$3.60 = \$1,693.80$

   The tax is $1,693.80

8. To find the tax rate based on a certain denomination when given the base and the tax derived:

   a. Divide the base by the denomination indicated.

   b. Divide the tax by this quotient.

   Example: Find the tax rate per $100 that would be required to raise $350,000 on $2,000,000 of taxable property.
   Solution: $2,000,000 ÷ $100 = 20,000
   $350,000 ÷ 20,000 = $17.50

   Tax rate = $17.50 per $100

9 Since a surtax is an additional tax besides the regular tax, to find the total tax:

   a. Change the regular tax rate to a decimal.

   b. Multiply the base by the regular tax rate.

   c. Change the surtax rate to a decimal.

   d. Multiply the base by the surtax rate.

   e. Add both taxes.

   Example: Assuming that the tax rate is 2⅓% on wines costing up to $3.00, and 3% on those costing from $3.00 to $6.00, and 3½% on those from $6.00 to $10.00, what would be the tax on a bottle costing $8.00 if there is a surtax of 5% on all wines above $5.00?
   Solution: An $8.00 bottle falls within the category of $6.00 to $10.00. The tax rate on such a bottle is

$$3\frac{1}{2}\% = .035$$
$$\$8.00 \times .035 = \$.28$$
$$\text{surtax rate} = 5\% = .05$$
$$\$8.00 \times .05 = \$.40$$
$$\$.28 + \$.40 = \$.68$$

$$\text{Total tax} = \$.68$$

Checking Accounts

Checks

```
ABC PRINTING CO., INC.                          268
378 Side Street
New York, N.Y. 12345              _____ 19_____

Pay to the _____ $_____
Order of
_____ Dollars

First Local Bank
100 Main St.
New York, N.Y. 11100             _____
        ⑆226070076⑆ 000
```

1. The form above is a typical check. The number in the upper right corner is the check number. This should not be confused with the account number, which is found in magnetic ink characters along the bottom of the check. Below the check number is space for the date. The name of the person to whom the check is made out is written in the space after

Pay to the order of. The amount of the check, in numbers, is written after the $, and the amount in words is written in the space before the word *dollars.* The person who is authorized to sign checks for the account signs in the lower right corner.

Example: Marion Silver writes a check to pay her rent of $475 to Home Realty Co. Her check appears below:

Deposits

2. Deposits to checking accounts are usually made using forms which are preprinted with the account name and number. Checks are listed separately from cash. Sometimes cash is separated into coin and currency (paper money).

   Example: Ira Schwartz makes a deposit of $15.82 in cash, and checks for $263.84, 68.54, and 386.52. His deposit slip is shown on the next page.

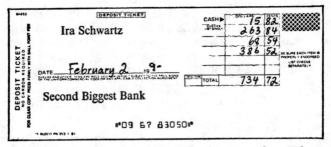

Example: At the end of the business day, Eileen prepares the deposit slip for Lader's Dress Shop. These amounts are to be deposited:

Checks: $83.25, 26.42, 97.65, 11.84, 73.90, 153.86, 267.14, 52.86

Currency: 14 twenty-dollar bills
57 ten-dollar bills
11 five-dollar bills
3 two-dollar bills
54 one-dollar bills

Coin: 57 quarters
39 dimes
84 nickels
17 pennies

She must first compute the amounts to be listed under *Currency* and *Coin.*

Currency: $14 \times \$20 = \$280$
$57 \times 10 = 570$
$11 \times 5 = 55$
$3 \times 2 = 6$
$54 \times 1 = \underline{54}$
Total currency $\$965$

Coin: $57 \times \$.25 = \$14.25$
        $39 \times\ \ .10 = \ \ \ 3.90$
        $84 \times\ \ .05 = \ \ \ 4.20$
        $17 \times\ \ .01 = \ \ \ \ \ .17$
        Total coins $22.52

The completed deposit slip is shown on the following page.

Computing the Balance

3. Whenever a check is drawn or a deposit is made, the amount must be recorded and the balance in the account adjusted accordingly. The amount of each check is subtracted from the balance, and the amount of each deposit is added to the balance. Ledgers or check stubs are provided with the checks for this purpose.

4. A check ledger is a booklet with space for recording transactions. It is separate from the checks themselves.

    Example: These transactions have been recorded in the double-line ledger at the top of page 143.

2/6	Balance	$562.85
2/6	Check #217 to	
	Home Realty	475.00
2/6	Deposit	734.92
2/10	Check #218 to	
	Lader's Dress Shop	26.42
2/12	Check #219 to	
	Dr. S. Healit	75.00

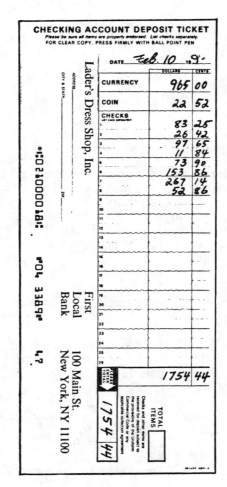

PLEASE BE SURE TO DEDUCT ANY PER CHECK CHARGES OR SERVICE CHARGES THAT MAY APPLY TO YOUR ACCOUNT							
CHECK NO	DATE	CHECKS ISSUED TO OR DESCRIPTION OF DEPOSIT	(-) AMOUNT OF CHECK	√ T	(-) CHECK FEE (IF ANY)	(+) AMOUNT OF DEPOSIT	BALANCE 562 85
217	2/6	Home Realty Co. (rent)	475 00				475 00
							87 85
	2/6					734 92	734 92
							822 77
218	2/10	Lader's Dress Shop	26 42				26 42
							796 35
219	2/12	Dr. S. Healit	75 00				75 00
							721 35

Notice that two lines are used for each transaction. The amount of the transaction is written below the balance, and the new balance is computed.

Example: Another form of ledger uses one line per transaction. Only the new balances are entered in the right-hand column. These balances have been computed elsewhere.

The same transactions as in the previous example have been recorded in this single-line ledger:

No.	Date	Description of Transaction	Amount	Balance 562 85
217	2/6	HOME REALTY Co	475 00	87 85
	2/6	Deposit	734 92	822 77
218	2/10	LADER'S DRESS SHOP	26 42	796 35
219	2/12	DR. S. HEALIT	75 00	721 35

5. Many businesses use check stubs to record transactions. After the check is written, it is removed from the checkbook by tearing through perforations, leaving the stub in the checkbook. In using the stubs, the new balance is calculated after each check is written.

Example: Dr. S. Healit's check stubs show these transactions:

3/8	Balance in account	$1896.75
3/8	Check #149 written to Laurie Brown (salary) for $186.50	
3/9	Check #150 written to I. Sweep Cleaning Service for $165.00	
3/9	Deposit of $785.50	
3/9	Check #151 written to *Today's Patient* magazine for $32.85	

An Illustration of the check stubs for these transactions appears on page 145.

6. In another form of checkbook, the balance is computed after a complete page of checks has been used.

Example: The record page illustrated on page 146 has been completed using the information in the previous example.

Check Stubs			
	Balance brought forward	1896	75

149

3/8 19 —

To *Laurie Brown*

For *salary*

} deposits

	Total	1896	75
	Amount this check	186	50
	Balance	1710	25

150

3/9 19 —

To *I. Sweep Cleaning*
For *Service*
Cleaning office

} deposits

	Total	1710	25
	Amount this check	165	00
	Balance	1545	25

151

3/9 19 —

To *Today's Patient*
For

magazine subscription

} deposits 185 | 50

	Total	2330	75
	Amount this check	32	85
	Balance	2297	90

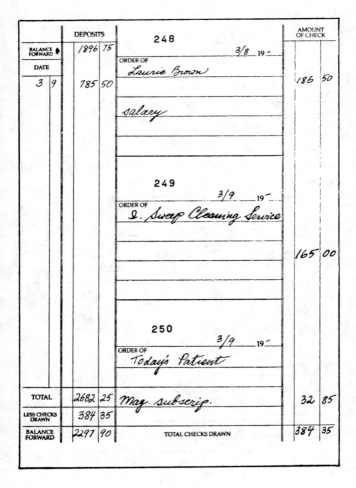

		DEPOSITS		248			AMOUNT OF CHECK	
BALANCE FORWARD ◆		1896	75			3/8 19–		
DATE				ORDER OF *Laurie Brown*			186	50
3	9	785	50					
				salary				
				249				
						3/9 19–		
				ORDER OF *I. Sweep Cleaning Service*				
							165	00
				250				
						3/9 19–		
				ORDER OF *Today's Patient*				
TOTAL		2682	25	*Mag. subscrip.*			32	85
LESS CHECKS DRAWN		384	35					
BALANCE FORWARD		2297	90	TOTAL CHECKS DRAWN			384	35

Bank Statements

7. a. At regular intervals the bank sends to each depositor a statement listing the transactions of the account. The statement must be compared (reconciled) with the records of the depositor. In reconciling the account, it is necessary to consider outstanding checks, deposits that were made too late to be shown on the statement, and service charges.

Example: In the bank statement shown on page 148, the checks (withdrawals) are listed in the order in which they were presented to the bank for payment. Other bank statements may have a different format but will show some listing of checks, deposits, and service charges—perhaps in a different order than this one does.

The records in the depositor's checkbook show a balance of $683.28. The bank statement and the depositor's records may be compared as follows:

Depositor		Bank	
Checkbook balance	683.28	Bank Statement balance	1196.35
Less		Less total of	
service charges	− 3.00	outstanding checks	− 716.07
Balance	680.28	Add late deposits	+ 200.00
		Balance	680.28

CHECKING ACCOUNT STATEMENT

Deposits	Withdrawals	Check Number/ Transaction	Date	Balance
		Starting balance	12/16	293.12
700.00		Deposit	12/17	993.12
	186.50	4302	12/20	806.62
	55.00	4303	12/22	751.62
	265.75	4304	12/22	485.87
	52.30	4306	12/22	433.57
	86.00	4308	12/24	347.57
239.80		Deposit	12/27	587.37
	27.54	4301	12/28	559.83
	12.96	4305	12/29	546.87
	263.50	4307	1/3	283.37
	75.00	4292	1/4	208.37
456.82		Deposit	1/5	665.19
	495.79	4300	1/6	169.40
852.89		Deposit	1/6	1022.29
	273.87	4315	1/6	748.42
	86.00	4310	1/12	662.42
	75.00	4316	1/13	587.42
798.43		Deposit	1/14	1385.85
	186.50	4314	1/15	1199.35
	3.00	Service charge	1/15	1196.35
		Closing balance	1/15	1196.35
3047.94		Total credits		
	2144.71	Total debits		

The depositor's records were adjusted by subtracting service charges which were shown on the statement but not yet noted in the checkbook ($3.00). The bank statement was adjusted as shown on page 147 by adding late deposits ($200.00) and subtracting all the checks that had not yet reached the bank for payment ($716.07).

b. Some banks provide reconciliation forms with their bank statements. A typical form, completed using the figures in the previous example, is shown on the following page.

CHECKING ACCOUNT RECONCILIATION

Closing Balance Shown on Front
   of Statement ....1 <u>1196.35</u>
Deposits and Credits Not Shown
   on this Statement:
       Date <u>1/15</u>   Amount <u>200.00</u>

Total Credits/Deposits Not
   Shown on this Statement ....2 <u>200.00</u>
Total of 1 and 2 ....3 <u>1396.35</u>
Outstanding Checks:
      Number <u>4309</u>   Amount <u>57.82</u>
          <u>4311</u>   <u>179.35</u>
          <u>4312</u>   <u>126.00</u>
          <u>4313</u>   <u>85.50</u>
          <u>4317</u>   <u>267.40</u>

Total Outstanding Checks ....4 <u>716.07</u>
Present Balance
   (Subtract 4 from 3) ....5 <u>680.28</u>
Balance in your Checkbook ....6 <u>683.28</u>
Service Charges and
   Miscellaneous Debits:
     <u>3.00</u>

           Total....................7 <u>3.00</u>
Adjusted Checkbook Balance
   (Subtract 7 from 6) ....8 <u>680.28</u>

The present balance (5) and your adjusted checkbook balance (8) should be equal.

8. a. Banks vary in the service charges applied to their accounts. There may be a monthly flat rate service charge, or the service charge may depend on the balance in the account. There may be a charge for each check written. Some banks charge for each deposit to the account and perhaps for each check within the deposit. Other charges are made for printing the checks, for checks that "bounce" (have insufficient funds in their accounts for payment), and for other returned checks. All of these charges must be subtracted as withdrawals in reconciling the account.

   b. Banks may pay interest on the balance in an account. This amount must be added as a deposit in reconciling the account.

Foreign Exchange

1. In order to compare United States money to the money of other countries, it is necessary to know the current foreign exchange rates. These rates change daily and may be found in the financial pages of many newspapers. The following is a typical foreign exchange table:

Foreign Exchange
Week ended December 17, 19—

	Foreign Currency in Dollars	Dollar in Foreign Currency
Argentina (Peso)	.000020	41640
Australia (Dollar)	.9722	1.0286
Austria (Schilling)	.0592	16.89
Belgium (Franc)	.0213	47.05
Bolivia (Peso)	.0227	44.00
Brazil (Cruzeiro)	.004225	236.66
Britain (Pound)	1.5960	.6266
Canada (Dollar)	.8073	1.2387
Denmark (Krone)	.1181	8.4650
Finland (Mark)	.1881	5.3170
France (Franc)	.1473	6.7900
Germany (Mark)	.4175	2.3950
Greece (Drachma)	.0142	70.50
Holland (Guilder)	.3781	2.6450
Italy (Lire)	.000723	1383.00
Japan (Yen)	.004200	238.00
Mexico (Peso)	.0105	95.00
Spain (Peseta)	.007880	126.95
Switzerland (Franc)	.4977	2.0090

2. To change an amount given in foreign currency to U.S. dollars, find the conversion number for the country you are interested in in the column headed *Foreign Currency in Dollars*. Multiply the given amount of money by the conversion number.

Example: Change 260 Mexican pesos to U.S. dollars.

Solution: In the table, the conversion number on the line for Mexico is .0105. This means that 1 peso = $.0105.

$$260 (\$.0105) = \$2.73$$
$$260 \text{ Mexican pesos} = \$2.73$$

3. To convert an amount given in U.S. dollars to a foreign currency, find the conversion number in the column headed *Dollar in Foreign Currency*. Multiply the given amount by the conversion number.

Example: Change $20 (U.S.) to Greek drachmas.

Solution: The conversion number in the table is 70.50. This means that $1 = 70.50 drachmas.

$$\$20(70.50) = 1410$$
$$\$20 = 1410 \text{ drachmas}$$

Postal Information

Independent Parcel Services
There is an ever-increasing number of independent delivery services which offer pick-up and delivery of correspondence and packages as an alternative to the U.S. Postal Service. Each offers special features with which to compete. You must investigate for yourself which of these services is active in your area and whether or not use of these alternatives is to your advantage.

The United States Postal Service
The following describes in detail costs and services offered by the U.S. Postal Service. Postal rates and regulations do change periodically. Check with your local post office for the most current information.

FIRST-CLASS MAIL

SINGLE-PIECE LETTER RATES

1st ounce	$0.29
Each additional ounce to 11 ounces	0.23
Over 11 ounces, see Priority Mail rates.	
Presort rates	See postmaster.
Business reply mail	See postmaster.

SIZE STANDARDS FOR DOMESTIC MAIL

MINIMUM SIZE

Pieces must meet the following requirements to be mailable:

a. All pieces must be at least 0.007 inch thick.
b. Pieces (except keys and identification devices) that are 1/4 inch or less thick must be:

(1) Rectangular in shape,
(2) At least 3 1/4 inches high, and
(3) At least 5 inches long.

c. Pieces greater than 1/4 inch thick can be mailed even if they measure less than 3 1/2 by 5 inches.

NONSTANDARD MAIL AND SURCHARGES

First-Class Mail (except Presort First-Class and carrier route First-Class weighing 1 ounce or less) and all single-piece rate third-class mail weighing 1 ounce or less are nonstandard (and subject to a $0.10 surcharge in addition to the applicable postage and fees) if:

a. Any of the following dimensions are exceeded:
(1) Length—11 1/2 inches,
(2) Height — 6 1/8 inches,
(3) Thickness — 1/4 inch, or

b. The length divided by the height (aspect ratio) is less than 1.3 or more than 2.5.

For nonstandard Presort First-Class and carrier route First Class, the surcharge is $0.05 in addition to applicable postage.

Priority Mail Rates

WEIGHT UP TO BUT NOT EXCEEDING POUND(S)	RATE					
	LOCAL ZONES 1-2-3	ZONE 4	ZONE 5	ZONE 6	ZONE 7	ZONE 8
2	$2.90 TO ALL ZONES					
3	$4.10 TO ALL ZONES					
4	$4.65 TO ALL ZONES					
5	$5.45 TO ALL ZONES					
6	$ 5.55	$ 5.75	$ 6.10	$ 6.85	$ 7.65	$ 8.60
7	5.70	6.10	6.70	7.55	8.50	9.65
8	5.90	6.50	7.30	8.30	9.40	10.70
9	6.10	7.00	7.95	9.05	10.25	11.75
10	6.35	7.55	8.55	9.80	11.15	12.80
11	6.75	8.05	9.20	10.55	12.05	13.80
12	7.15	8.55	9.80	11.30	12.90	14.85
13	7.50	9.10	10.40	12.05	13.80	15.90
14	7.90	9.60	11.05	12.80	14.65	16.95
15	8.30	10.10	11.65	13.55	15.55	18.00
16	8.70	10.65	12.30	14.30	16.45	19.05
17	9.10	11.15	12.90	15.05	17.30	20.10
18	9.50	11.65	13.55	15.80	18.20	21.10
19	9.90	12.20	14.15	16.50	19.05	22.15
20	10.30	12.70	14.75	17.25	19.95	23.20
21	10.70	13.25	15.40	18.00	20.85	24.25
22	11.10	13.75	16.00	18.75	21.70	25.30
23	11.50	14.25	16.65	19.50	22.60	26.35
24	11.90	14.80	17.25	20.25	23.45	27.40
25	12.30	15.30	17.90	21.00	24.35	28.45
26	12.70	15.80	18.50	21.75	25.25	29.45
27	13.10	16.35	19.10	22.50	26.10	30.50
28	13.50	16.85	19.75	23.25	27.00	31.55
29	13.90	17.35	20.35	24.00	27.85	32.60
30	14.30	17.90	21.00	24.75	28.75	33.65
31	14.70	18.40	21.60	25.50	29.65	34.70
32	15.10	18.95	22.20	26.20	30.50	35.75
33	15.50	19.45	22.85	26.95	31.40	36.75
34	15.90	19.95	23.45	27.70	32.25	37.80
35	16.30	20.50	24.10	28.45	33.15	38.85
36	16.70	21.00	24.70	29.20	34.05	39.90
37	17.10	21.50	25.35	29.95	34.90	40.95
38	17.45	22.05	25.95	30.70	35.80	42.00
39	17.85	22.55	26.55	31.45	36.65	43.05
40	18.25	23.05	27.20	32.20	37.55	44.05
41	18.65	23.60	27.80	32.95	38.45	45.10
42	19.05	24.10	28.45	33.70	39.30	46.15

WEIGHT UP TO BUT NOT EXCEEDING POUND(S)	RATE					
	LOCAL ZONES 1-2-3	ZONE 4	ZONE 5	ZONE 6	ZONE 7	ZONE 8
43	$19.45	$24.60	$29.05	$34.45	$40.20	$47.20
44	19.85	25.15	29.65	35.15	41.05	48.25
45	20.25	25.65	30.30	35.90	41.95	49.30
46	20.65	26.20	30.90	36.65	42.85	50.35
47	21.05	26.70	31.55	37.40	43.70	51.35
48	21.45	27.20	32.15	38.15	44.60	52.40
49	21.85	27.75	32.80	38.90	45.45	53.45
50	22.25	28.25	33.40	39.65	46.35	54.50
51	22.65	28.75	34.00	40.40	47.25	55.55
52	23.05	29.30	34.65	41.15	48.10	56.60
53	23.45	29.80	35.25	41.90	49.00	57.65
54	23.85	30.30	35.90	42.65	49.85	58.65
55	24.25	30.85	36.50	43.40	50.75	59.70
56	24.65	31.35	37.15	44.15	51.65	60.75
57	25.05	31.90	37.75	44.85	52.50	61.80
58	25.45	32.40	38.35	45.60	53.40	62.85
59	25.85	32.90	39.00	46.35	54.25	63.90
60	26.25	33.45	39.60	47.10	55.15	64.95
61	26.65	33.95	40.25	47.85	56.05	65.95
62	27.05	34.45	40.85	48.60	56.90	67.00
63	27.40	35.00	41.45	49.35	57.80	68.05
64	27.80	35.50	42.10	50.10	58.65	69.10
65	28.20	36.00	42.70	50.85	59.55	70.15
66	28.60	36.55	43.35	51.60	60.45	71.20
67	29.00	37.05	43.95	52.35	61.30	72.25
68	29.40	37.55	44.60	53.10	62.20	73.25
69	29.80	38.10	45.20	53.80	63.05	74.30
70	30.20	38.60	45.80	54.55	63.95	75.35

NOTES: 1. The 2-pound rate is charged for matter sent in a "flat rate" envelope provided by the Postal Service.
2. Add $4.50 for each pickup stop.
3. Pieces presented in mailings of at least 300 pieces and meeting applicable Postal Service regulations for presorted Priority Mail receive a 10-cent per piece discount.
4. Exception: Parcels weighing less than 15 pounds but measuring more than 84 inches in length and girth combined are chargeable with a minimum rate equal to that for a 15-pound parcel for the zone to which addressed.

Second-Class Mail

Regular and preferred second-class rates are available only to newspapers and periodicals that have been authorized second-class privileges.

Third-Class Mail

Third-class mail is specific types of matter — circulars, books, catalogs, and other printed material; merchandise; seeds, cuttings, bulbs, roots, scions, and plants — weighing less than 16 ounces.

REGULAR AND SPECIAL BULK RATES AVAILABLE ONLY TO AUTHORIZED MAILERS

See postmaster for details.

Fourth-Class Mail

PARCEL POST ZONED RATES

See postmaster for weight and size limits.

PARCEL POST PICKUP

$4.50 is charged for each pickup stop.

Wherever the mailing rate is based upon distance, the distance is calculated by a zone rate chart. The Postal Service issues zone charts specific to locations with clusters of zip codes. The zone chart on the next page applies only to mail originating from the specified zip codes. You must request from your local post office the zone chart that applies to your own business location.

U.S. POSTAL SERVICE OFFICIAL ZONE CHART

ORIGINATING FROM ZIP CODES BEGINNING
WITH: 004-005, 105, 107-108, 114-115, 117-118

Zip Code Prefixes	Zone	Zip Code Prefixes	Zone	Zip Code Prefixes	Zone	Zip Code Prefixes	Zone
004-005	1	160-162	4	390-392	6	640-649	6
006-009	7	163	3	393	5	650-652	5
010-013	2	164-165	4	394-396	6	653	6
014	3	166-169	3	397-402	5	654-655	5
015-018	2	170-172	2	403-406	4	656-676	6
019	3	173-174	3	407-409	5	677-679	7
020-024	2	175-176	2	410-418	4	680-689	6
025-026	3	177	3	420-427	5	690	7
027-029	2	178-199	2	430-459	4	691-692	6
030-033	3	200-218	3	460-466	5	693	7
034	2	219	2	467-468	4	700-722	6
035-043	3	220-238	3	469	5	723-724	5
044	4	239-253	4	470	4	725-732	6
045	3	254	3	471-472	5	733	7
046-049	4	255-266	4	473	4	734-738	6
050-051	3	267	3	474-479	5	739	7
052-053	2	268-288	4	480-489	4	740-762	6
054	3	289-292	5	490-491	5	763-772	7
055	2	293	4	492	4	773	6
056-059	3	294	5	493-499	5	774-775	7
060-063	2	295-297	4	500-503	6	776-777	6
064-066	1	298-324	5	504	5	778-797	7
067	2	325	6	505	6	798-799	8
068-079	1	326-329	5	506-507	5	800-812	7
080-084	2	330-334	6	508-516	6	813	8
085-119	1	335-336	5	520-539	5	814	7
120-127	2	337	6	540	6	815	8
128-136	3	338	5	541-549	5	816-820	7
137-139	2	339-341	6	550-555	6	821	8
140-142	3	342-364	5	556-559	5	822-828	7
143	4	365-366	6	560-576	6	829-874	8
144-149	3	367-375	5	577	7	875-877	7
150-154	4	376	4	580-585	6	878-880	8
155	3	377-386	5	586-593	7	881-884	7
156	4	387	6	594-599	8	890-999	8
157-159	3	388-389	5	600-639	5		

The local rate applies to all parcels mailed at a post office or on its rural routes for delivery at that office or on its rural routes.

PARCEL POST RATES*
FOURTH-CLASS MAIL

Weight up to but not exceeding (pounds)	ZONES							
	Local	1&2	3	4	5	6	7	8
2	$2.12	$2.19	$2.32	$2.46	$2.74	$2.85	$2.85	$2.85
3	2.19	2.29	2.49	2.70	3.12	3.54	4.00	4.05
4	2.25	2.39	2.65	2.94	3.50	4.06	4.35	4.60
5	2.31	2.49	2.81	3.17	3.88	4.58	5.20	5.40
6	2.38	2.59	2.98	3.41	4.26	5.10	6.33	8.55
7	2.44	2.68	3.14	3.65	4.64	5.62	7.06	9.60
8	2.50	2.78	3.31	3.89	5.02	6.14	7.78	10.65
9	2.57	2.88	3.47	4.12	5.40	6.67	8.51	11.70
10	2.63	2.98	3.63	4.36	5.78	7.19	9.24	12.75
11	2.69	3.08	3.80	4.60	6.16	7.71	9.97	13.75
12	2.76	3.18	3.96	4.83	6.54	8.23	10.69	14.80
13	2.80	3.25	4.08	4.99	6.79	8.57	11.17	15.85
14	2.85	3.32	4.18	5.16	7.04	8.92	11.65	16.90
15	2.89	3.38	4.28	5.27	7.23	9.17	11.99	17.95
16	2.93	3.43	4.36	5.39	7.40	9.40	12.31	19.00
17	2.97	3.48	4.44	5.49	7.56	9.62	12.61	19.91
18	3.01	3.53	4.51	5.60	7.72	9.83	12.90	20.38
19	3.05	3.58	4.59	5.69	7.87	10.03	13.17	20.83
20	3.08	3.63	4.65	5.79	8.01	10.22	13.43	21.26
21	3.12	3.68	4.72	5.88	8.15	10.40	13.68	21.66
22	3.15	3.72	4.79	5.97	8.28	10.57	13.91	22.05
23	3.18	3.77	4.85	6.05	8.40	10.74	14.14	22.43
24	3.22	3.81	4.91	6.13	8.52	10.90	14.36	22.78
25	3.25	3.85	4.97	6.21	8.64	11.05	14.57	23.13
26	3.28	3.89	5.03	6.29	8.76	11.20	14.77	23.46
27	3.32	3.93	5.09	6.36	8.87	11.35	14.97	23.78
28	3.35	3.97	5.14	6.44	8.97	11.49	15.16	24.09
29	3.38	4.01	5.20	6.51	9.08	11.63	15.34	24.39
30	3.41	4.05	5.25	6.58	9.18	11.76	15.52	24.68
31	3.44	4.09	5.30	6.65	9.28	11.89	15.69	24.96
32	3.47	4.13	5.36	6.71	9.37	12.01	15.86	25.23
33	3.50	4.17	5.41	6.78	9.47	12.14	16.02	25.50
34	3.53	4.20	5.46	6.84	9.56	12.26	16.18	25.75
35	3.56	4.24	5.51	6.91	9.65	12.37	16.34	26.01

Weight up to but not exceeding (pounds)	ZONES							
	Local	1&2	3	4	5	6	7	8
36	$3.59	$4.28	$5.55	$6.97	$9.74	$12.49	$16.49	$26.25
37	3.62	4.31	5.60	7.03	9.82	12.60	16.64	26.49
38	3.65	4.35	5.65	7.09	9.91	12.71	16.79	26.72
39	3.68	4.38	5.69	7.15	9.99	12.81	16.93	26.95
40	3.71	4.42	5.74	7.20	10.07	12.92	17.07	27.17
41	3.74	4.45	5.78	7.26	10.15	13.02	17.20	27.39
42	3.77	4.48	5.83	7.32	10.23	13.12	17.33	27.60
43	3.79	4.52	5.87	7.37	10.31	13.22	17.47	27.81
44	3.82	4.55	5.92	7.43	10.38	13.32	17.59	28.01
45	3.85	4.58	5.96	7.48	10.46	13.41	17.72	28.21
46	3.88	4.62	6.00	7.53	10.53	13.51	17.84	28.41
47	3.91	4.65	6.04	7.58	10.60	13.60	17.96	28.60
48	3.93	4.68	6.09	7.64	10.67	13.69	18.08	28.79
49	3.96	4.72	6.13	7.69	10.74	13.78	18.20	28.97
50	3.99	4.75	6.17	7.74	10.81	13.87	18.32	29.15
51	4.02	4.78	6.21	7.79	10.88	13.95	18.43	29.33
52	4.04	4.81	6.25	7.84	10.95	14.04	18.54	29.51
53	4.07	4.84	6.29	7.89	11.01	14.12	18.65	29.68
54	4.10	4.87	6.33	7.93	11.08	14.21	18.76	29.85
55	4.12	4.91	6.37	7.98	11.15	14.29	18.86	30.02
56	4.15	4.94	6.41	8.03	11.21	14.37	18.97	30.18
57	4.18	4.97	6.44	8.08	11.27	14.45	19.07	30.34
58	4.20	5.00	6.48	8.12	11.34	14.53	19.18	30.50
59	4.23	5.03	6.52	8.17	11.40	14.61	19.28	30.66
60	4.26	5.06	6.56	8.21	11.46	14.68	19.38	30.81
61	4.28	5.09	6.59	8.26	11.52	14.76	19.47	30.97
62	4.31	5.12	6.63	8.30	11.58	14.83	19.57	31.12
63	4.34	5.15	6.67	8.35	11.64	14.91	19.67	31.27
64	4.36	5.18	6.71	8.39	11.70	14.98	19.76	31.41
65	4.39	5.21	6.74	8.44	11.76	15.05	19.86	31.56
66	4.42	5.24	6.78	8.48	11.81	15.13	19.95	31.70
67	4.44	5.27	6.81	8.52	11.87	15.20	20.04	31.84
68	4.47	5.30	6.85	8.57	11.93	15.27	20.13	31.98
69	4.49	5.33	6.89	8.61	11.98	15.34	20.22	32.12
70	4.52	5.36	6.92	8.65	12.04	15.41	20.31	32.25

*See postmaster for parcel airlift (PAL), space available mail (SAM), bound printed matter, special fourth-class, and library rates

EXPRESS MAIL

An overnight delivery service that's fast, reliable, convenient, and economical.

Availability. Express Mail Service is available 7 days a week, 365 days a year (at no additional charge) for mailable items up to 70 pounds in weight or 108 inches in combined length and girth. Call 1-800-333-8777 for our convenient pickup service — one low fee of $4.50, no matter how many pieces.

Letter rates of $9.95 (up to 8 ounces) and $13.95 (up to 2 pounds) for Post Office to Addressee service. For rates exceeding 2 pounds and up to the 70-pound limit, consult your postmaster. Rates vary for other types of Express Mail services, which include Post Office to Post Office, Same Day Airport service, and Custom Designed Service.

Convenient flat-rate envelope. No need to stand in line at the post office to have your item weighed. No matter what the item weighs, it all goes for the same low 2-pound rate. Just use the Express Mail flat-rate envelope, pay the appropriate 2-pound postage rate for the level of service desired (use stamps, meter strips, or your Express Mail Corporate Account), and put your documents into the flat-rate envelope. To mail your item, call for a pickup or hand it to your postal carrier. For Post Office to Post Office or Post Office to Addressee services, you may drop the item into any Express Mail box.

Service features. Features include: noon delivery between major business markets, merchandise and document reconstruction insurance; Express Mail shipping containers; shipment receipts; special collection boxes; and such options as return receipt service, COD service, waiver of signature, and pickup service.

See postmaster or account representative for additional information on other Express Mail services (such as military and international) and a copy of your local Express Mail network directory.

Refunds. The Postal Service will refund, upon application to the originating office, the postage for any Express Mail shipments not meeting the service standard, except for those delayed by strike or work stoppage.

SPECIAL SERVICES

CERTIFIED MAIL
Receipt and delivery record at destination post office

Class of Mail	Fee in addition to postage
First-Class and Priority Mail only	$1.00

COD (Collect on Delivery)
The maximum value for COD service is $600.00.
See postmaster for fees and conditions of mailing.

INSURANCE
Coverage against loss or damage

Liability	Fee in addition to postage
$ 0.01 to 50.00	$0.75
50.01 to 100.00	1.60
100.01 to 200.00	2.40
200.01 to 300.00	3.50
300.01 to 400.00	4.60
400.01 to 500.00	5.40
500.01 to 600.00	6.20

REGISTRY
Maximum protection and security

Value	Article covered by postal insurance	Article not covered by postal insurance
$ 0.01 to 100.00	$4.50	$4.40
100.01 to 500.00	4.85	4.70
500.01 to 1,000.00	5.25	5.05
For higher values, see postmaster.		

Fee in addition to postage

SPECIAL DELIVERY
Expedited delivery at destination

Class of Mail	2 pounds or less	More than 2 pounds but not more than 10 pounds	More than 10 pounds
First-class	$7.65	$7.95	$8.55
All others	8.05	8.65	9.30

Fee in addition to postage

SPECIAL HANDLING Third- and fourth-class mail only	
Weight	**Fee in addition to postage**
10 pounds and less	$1.80
More than 10 pounds	2.50
ADDITIONAL SERVICES	
Service	**Fee in addition to postage**
CERTIFICATE OF MAILING .... (For bulk mailings and firm mailing books, see postmaster)	$0.50

RETURN RECEIPT
(Available for COD, Express Mail, certified,
insured (if more than $50), and registered mail)
• REQUESTED AT TIME OF MAILING
  Showing to whom (signature)
  and date delivered ....
 	
  Showing to whom (signature),
  date, and address where delivered ....
• REQUESTED AFTER MAILING
  Showing to whom and date delivered .....
• RESTRICTED DELIVERY
  (Available for COD, certified, insured,
  and registered mail.) ....
	
	$1.00
	
	1.35
	
	6.00
	
	2.50

RETURN RECEIPT FOR MERCHANDISE
(Without another special service)
• Showing to whom (signature)
  and date delivered ....
• Showing to whom (signature), date,
  and address where delivered ....
	
	$1.10
	
	1.50

Money Orders

Amount of Money Order	Fee
$0.01 to 700.00	$0.75

TEST YOUR UNDERSTANDING

PRACTICE PROBLEMS

The problems that follow will give you a chance to apply your new-found mathematical knowledge. Detailed solutions follow the last problem to illustrate the reasoning involved and to help you assess your own problem-solving ability.

1. A bag of nickels and dimes contains $11.50. If there are 73 dimes, how many nickels are there?
   (A) 78   (C) 82
   (B) 80   (D) 84

2. A shipment consists of 340 ten-foot pieces of conduit with a coupling on each piece. If the conduit weighs 0.85 lb per foot and each coupling weighs 0.15 lb, the total weight of the shipment is
   (A) 340 lb   (C) 2941 lb
   (B) 628 lb   (D) 3400 lb

3. A carton contains 9 dozen file folders. If a clerk removes 53 folders, how many are left in the carton?
   (A) 37   (C) 55
   (B) 44   (D) 62

4. What tax rate on a base of $4782 would yield $286.92?
   (A) 6%
   (B) 8¼%
   (C) 12%
   (D) 16⅔%

5. Two adjacent walls of a 40' by 35' office are to be painted. The walls are 8' high and include no doors or windows. If each gallon of the paint to be used covers 450 square feet, how many gallons are needed?
   (A) 1⅓
   (B) 1½
   (C) 2⅓
   (D) 2½

6. The difference between one tenth of 2000 and one-tenth percent of 2000 is
   (A) 0
   (B) 18
   (C) 180
   (D) 198

7. If the fractions 5/7, ½, ⅗, and ⅔ are arranged in ascending order of size, the result is
   (A) ½, ⅗, ⅔, 5/7
   (B) ⅗, 5/7, ⅔, ½
   (C) ½, ⅔, ⅗, 5/7
   (D) 5/7, ⅔, ⅗, ½

8. An employee has 2/9 of his salary withheld for income tax. The percent of his salary that is withheld is most nearly
   (A) 16%
   (B) 18%
   (C) 20%
   (D) 22%

9. The value of 3 + 5(6 − 4) is
   (A) 13
   (B) 16
   (C) 29
   (D) none of these

10. A driver traveled 100 miles at the rate of 40 mph, then traveled 80 miles at 60 mph. The total number of hours for the entire trip was
    (A) 1³⁄₂₀   (C) 2¼
    (B) 1¾   (D) 3⅚

11. Of the following readings of rainfall—1.2 inches, 2.4 inches, 2.2 inches, 3.5 inches, 4.3 inches, 2.3 inches, 4.2 inches, 3.9 inches, 3.0 inches, 3.3 inches, 2.9 inches, 3.6 inches, 4.5 inches, 4.7 inches, and 4.6 inches—the median is
    (A) 3.5   (C) 3.4
    (B) 3.3   (D) 3.0

12. The single commercial discount that is equivalent to successive discounts of 10% and 10% is
    (A) 20%   (C) 17%
    (B) 19%   (D) 15%

13. After an article is discounted at 25%, it sells for $375. The original price of the article was
    (A) $93.75   (C) $375
    (B) $350   (D) $500

14. If Mr. Mitchell has $627.04 in his checking account and then writes three checks for $241.75, $13.24, and $102.97, what will be his new balance?
    (A) $257.88   (C) $357.96
    (B) $269.08   (D) $369.96

15. If erasers cost 8¢ each for the first 250, 7¢ each for the next 250, and 5¢ for every eraser thereafter,

how many erasers may be purchased for $50?
(A) 600   (C) 850
(B) 750   (D) 1000

16. Assume that it is necessary to partition a room
measuring 40 feet by 20 feet into eight smaller
rooms of equal size. Allowing no room for aisles,
the *minimum* amount of partitioning that would be
needed is
(A) 90 ft   (C) 110 ft
(B) 100 ft   (D) 140 ft

17. As a result of reports received by the Housing Au-
thority concerning the reputed ineligibility of 756
tenants because of above-standard incomes, an in-
tensive check of their employers has been ordered.
Four housing assistants have been assigned to this
task. At the end of 6 days at 7 hours each, they have
checked on 336 tenants. In order to speed up the
investigation, two more housing assistants are assigned at this point. If they worked at the same rate,
the number of additional 7-hour days it would take
to complete the job is, most nearly,
(A) 1   (C) 5
(B) 3   (D) 7

18. A plane left New York at 3:30 p.m. EST and ar-
rived in Los Angeles at 4:15 p.m. PST. How long
did the flight take?
(A) 7 hrs 15 min   (C) 3 hrs 45 min
(B) 6 hrs 45 min   (D) 3 hrs 15 min

19. A parcel delivery service charges $9.26 for the first 4
pounds of package weight and an additional $1.06

for each half-pound over 4 pounds. What is the charge for a package weighing 6½ pounds?

(A) $2.65   (C) $11.91
(B) $6.89   (D) $14.56

20. 7⅔% of $1200 is
(A) $87   (C) $112
(B) $92   (D) $920

21. A certain family spends 30% of its income for food, 8% for clothing, 25% for shelter, 4% for recreation, 13% for education, and 5% for miscellaneous items. The weekly earnings are $500. What is the number of weeks it would take this family to save $15,000?
(A) 100   (C) 175
(B) 150   (D) 200

22. The value of forty thousand nickels is
(A) $20   (C) $2000
(B) $200   (D) $20,000

23. A cab driver works on a commission basis, receiving 42½% of the fares. In addition, his earnings from tips are valued at 29% of the commissions. If his average weekly fares equal $520, then his monthly earnings are
(A) between $900 and $1000
(B) between $1000 and $1100
(C) between $1100 and $1200
(D) over $1200

24. The terms on an invoice dated 3/18 are n/15. By
what date is full payment due?
(A) March 31   (C) April 15
(B) April 2   (D) April 18

25. What is the total cost of 3 sheets of 20¢ stamps, 2
sheets of 13¢ stamps, and 4 sheets of 17¢ stamps, if
each sheet has 100 stamps?
(A) $76.00   (C) $154.00
(B) $98.00   (D) $186.00

26. An employee's net pay is equal to his total earnings
less all deductions. If an employee's total earnings
in a pay period are $497.05, what is his net pay if he
has the following deductions: federal income tax,
$90.32; FICA, $30.82; Medicare, $7.21; state tax,
$18.79; city tax, $7.25; pension, $1.88?
(A) $341.89   (C) $340.89
(B) $341.78   (D) $340.78

27. Assume that two types of files have been ordered:
200 of type A and 100 of type B. When the files are
delivered, the buyer discovers that 25% of each
type is damaged. Of the remaining files, 20% of
type A and 40% of type B are the wrong color. The
total number of files that are the wrong color is
(A) 30   (C) 50
(B) 40   (D) 60

28. A parade is marching up an avenue for 60 city
blocks. A sample count of the number of people
watching the parade is taken, first in a block near
the end of the parade, and then in a block at the

middle. The former count is 4000, the latter is 6000. If the average for the entire parade is assumed to be the average of the two samples, then the estimated number of persons watching the entire parade is most nearly

(A) 240,000   (C) 480,000
(B) 300,000   (D) 600,000

29. A train ticket costs 138 guilders. If the exchange rate is 1 guilder = $.3815, what is the price of the ticket in dollars (to the nearest cent)?

(A) $38.15   (C) $138.15
(B) $52.65   (D) $361.73

30. The total length of fencing needed to enclose a rectangular area 46 feet by 34 feet is

(A) 26 yd 1 ft   (C) 52 yd 2 ft
(B) $26\frac{2}{3}$ yd   (D) $53\frac{1}{3}$ yd

31. Find the length of time it would take $432 to yield $74.52 in interest at $5\frac{3}{4}\%$ per annum.

(A) 2 yr 10 mo   (C) 3 yr 10 mo
(B) 3 yr   (D) 4 yr

32. The price of a radio is $31.29, which includes a 5% sales tax. What was the price of the radio before the tax was added?

(A) $29.80   (C) $29.90
(B) $29.85   (D) $29.95

33 If a person in the 15% income tax bracket paid $2775 in income taxes, his taxable income was

(A) $18,500   (C) $53,800
(B) $32,763   (D) $67,785

34. Of the numbers 6, 5, 3, 3, 6, 3, 4, 3, 4, 3, the mode
    is
    (A) 3   (C) 5
    (B) 4   (D) 6

Questions 35 and 36 refer to the following graph:

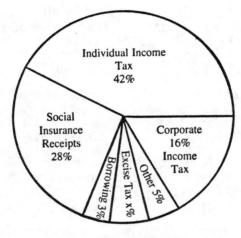

**Origin of Federal Revenues
of $352.6 Billion**

35. The total individual income tax and corporate in-
    come tax revenues were, to the nearest billion dol-
    lars,
    (A) 58   (C) 205
    (B) 123   (D) 256

36. The revenue from excise tax was, to the nearest billion dollars,
    (A) 14   (C) 20
    (B) 15   (D) 21

37. In a group of 100 people, 37 wear glasses. What is the probability that a person chosen at random from this group does *not* wear glasses?
    (A) .37   (C) .63
    (B) .50   (D) 1.00

38. The interest on $148.00 at 6% for 60 days is
    (A) $8.88   (C) $14.80
    (B) $2.96   (D) $ 1.48

39. A man bought a camera that was listed at $160. He was given successive discounts of 20% and 10%. The price he paid was
    (A) $112.00   (C) $119.60
    (B) $115.20   (D) $129.60

40. The water level of a swimming pool measuring 75 feet by 42 feet is to be raised four inches. If there are 7.48 gallons in a cubic foot, the number of gallons of water that will be needed is
    (A) 140   (C) 7854
    (B) 31,500   (D) 94,500

41. A salesman is paid 4½% commission on his first $7000 of sales and 5½% commission on all sales in excess of $7000. If his sales were $9600, how much commission did he earn?
    (A) $432   (C) $480
    (B) $458   (D) $528

42. How many boxes 3 inches by 4 inches by 5 inches
can fit into a carton 3 feet by 4 feet by 5 feet?
(A) 60   (C) 1728
(B) 144   (D) 8640

43. The value of 32 nickels, 73 quarters, and 156 dimes
is
(A) $26.10   (C) $35.45
(B) $31.75   (D) $49.85

44. Change 1855 on a 24-hour clock to 12-hour clock
time.
(A) 6:55 a.m.   (C) 8:55 a.m.
(B) 6:55 p.m.   (D) 8:55 p.m.

45. The wage rate in a certain trade is $8.60 an hour for
a 40-hour week and 1½ times the base pay for overtime. An employee who works 48 hours in a week
earns
(A) $447.20   (C) $582.20
(B) $498.20   (D) $619.20

46. Jane Michaels borrowed $200 on March 31 at the
simple interest rate of 8% per year. If she wishes to
repay the loan and the interest on May 15, what is
the total amount she must pay?
(A) $201   (C) $203
(B) $202   (D) $204

47. How many decigrams are in .57 kilograms?
(A) 57   (C) 5700
(B) 570   (D) 57,000

48. If candies are bought at $1.10 per dozen and sold at 3 for 55 cents, the total profit on 5½ dozen is
    (A) $5.55   (C) $6.55
    (B) $6.05   (D) $7.05

49. Airline regulations allow 20 kilograms of luggage per passenger. What is this equivalent to in pounds?
    (A) 9   (C) 44
    (B) 22   (D) 45

50. The owner of a stationery store bought binders at $16.00 per dozen. At what price must he sell each binder if he wants to realize a profit of 35% of his cost?
    (A) $1.65   (C) $1.80
    (B) $1.76   (D) $1.95

Solutions to Practice Problems

1.   73 dimes = 73 × $.10
                     = $7.30
    $11.50 − $7.30 = $4.20
    There is $4.20 worth of nickels in the bag.
        $4.20 ÷ $.05 = 84 nickels

    Answer: **(D)** 84

2. Each 10-foot piece weighs
   10 × .85 lb =   8.5 lb
                  + .15 lb
                    ‾‾‾‾‾‾‾
                    8.65 lb

The entire shipment weighs
340 × 8.65 lb = 2941 lb

Answer: **(C)**   2941 lb

3.   The carton contains 9 × 12 = 108 folders.
108 − 53 = 55 remain in carton
Answer: **(C)**   55

4.   Rate = tax ÷ base

$$286.92 \div 4782 = 4782\overline{)286.92}^{\,.06}$$
$$\underline{286\ 92}$$
$$.06 = 6\%$$

Answer: **(A)**   6%

5.   Area of 40′ wall = 40′ × 8′ =   320 sq ft
Area of 35′ wall = 35′ × 8′ = + 280 sq ft
                    Total area =   600 sq ft
600 ÷ 450 = 1⅓ gallons

Answer: **(A)**   1⅓

6.   ¹/₁₀ of 2000 = ¹/₁₀ × 2000 = 200
¹/₁₀% of 2000 = .001 × 2000 = 2
The difference is 200 − 2 = 198.

Answer: **(D)**   198

7.   To compare the fractions, change them to fractions
having the same denominator.
         L.C.D. = 7 × 2 × 5 × 3 = 210

$$5/7 = {}^{150}\!/_{210}$$
$$1/2 = {}^{105}\!/_{210}$$
$$3/5 = {}^{126}\!/_{210}$$
$$2/3 = {}^{140}\!/_{210}$$

The correct order is ${}^{105}\!/_{210}$, ${}^{126}\!/_{210}$, ${}^{140}\!/_{210}$, ${}^{150}\!/_{210}$.

Answer: **(A)**   ½, ⅗, ⅔, 5/7

8.
$$2/9 = 9\overline{)2.00} \quad .22\tfrac{2}{9}$$
$$\underline{1\ 8}$$
$$20$$
$$\underline{18}$$
$$2$$

$.22\tfrac{2}{9} = 22\%$ approximately

Answer: **(D)**   22%

9. $3 + 5(6 - 4) = 3 + 5(2)$
$$= 3 + 10$$
$$= 13$$

Answer: **(A)**   13

10.   The first part of the trip took
$$100 \text{ mi} \div 40 \text{ mph} = 2\tfrac{1}{2} \text{ hours}$$
The second part of the trip took
$$80 \text{ mi} \div 60 \text{ mph} = 1\tfrac{1}{3} \text{ hours}$$
$$2\tfrac{1}{2} = 2\tfrac{3}{6}$$
$$\underline{+\ 1\tfrac{1}{3}} = \underline{+\ 1\tfrac{2}{6}}$$
$$3\tfrac{5}{6}$$

Answer: **(D)**   3⅚

11. To find the median, arrange the values in order:
1.2, 2.2, 2.3, 2.4, 2.9,
3.0, 3.3, 3.5, 3.6, 3.9,
4.2, 4.3, 4.5, 4.6, 4.7
The median is the middle value in the list, or **3.5.**

Answer: **(A)** 3.5

12. Subtract 10%   100%
   of 100%:   − 10%
Subtract 10%   90%
   of 90%:   −   9%
                       81%
100% − 81% = 19% single equivalent discount

Answer: **(B)** 19%

13. $375 is 75% of the original price.
The original price = $375 ÷ 75%
                     = $375 ÷ .75
                     = $500

Answer: **(D)** $500

14. Total of checks: $241.75
                       13.24
               + 102.97
                 $357.96
  $627.04 old balance
 − 357.96 checks
  $269.08 new balance

Answer: **(B)** $269.08

15. First 250 erasers:
$$250 \times \$.08 = \$20.00$$
Next 250 erasers:
$$250 \times \$.07 = \$17.50$$
Total for 500 erasers:
$$\$20.00 + \$17.50 = \$37.50$$
$$\$50.00 - \$37.50 = \$12.50$$
$12.50 remains for 5¢ erasers:
$$\$12.50 \div \$.05 = 250 \text{ erasers}$$
$$500 + 250 = 750$$

Answer: **(B)** 750

16. The room may be partitioned as is shown below:

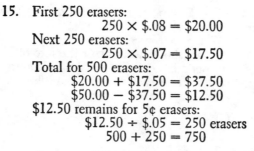

The total amount of partitioning is 100 feet.

Answer: **(B)** 100 ft

17. Four assistants completed 336 cases in 42 hours (6 days at 7 hours per day). Therefore, each assistant completed 336 ÷ 4, or 84 cases in 42 hours, for a rate of 2 cases per hour per assistant.

After the first 6 days, the number of cases remaining is
$$756 - 336 = 420$$
It will take 6 assistants, working at the rate of 2
cases per hour per assistant, $420 \div 12$ or 35 hours
to complete the work. If each workday has 7 hours,
then $35 \div 7$ or 5 days are needed.

Answer: **(C)**   5

18.   4:15 PST = 7:15 EST

$$
\begin{array}{ll}
\overset{6\ 7}{7:\cancel{1}5} & \text{arrived} \\
\underline{3:30} & \text{departed} \\
3:45 &
\end{array}
$$

Answer: **(C)**   3 hours 45 minutes

19.   6½ pounds − 4 pounds = 2½ pounds
$$2\tfrac{1}{2} \div \tfrac{1}{2} = 5$$
There are 5 half-pounds in 2½ pounds.
$$
\begin{aligned}
\$9.26 + 5(1.06) &= \$9.26 + 5.30 \\
&= \$14.56
\end{aligned}
$$

Answer: **(D)**   \$14.56

20.   7⅔% of \$1200 = ²³⁄₃% of \$1200
To change ²³⁄₃% to a fraction, divide by 100:
$$\tfrac{23}{3} \div 100 = \tfrac{23}{3} \times \tfrac{1}{100} = \tfrac{23}{300}$$

$$\overset{4}{\cancel{\tfrac{23}{300}}} \times \$\cancel{1200} = \$92$$

Answer: **(B)**   \$92

21. The family spends a total of 85% of its income. Therefore, 100% − 85%, or 15%, remains for savings.

$$15\% \text{ of } \$500 = .15 \times \$500$$
$$= \$75 \text{ per week}$$
$$\$15,000 \div \$75 = 200 \text{ weeks}$$

Answer: **(D)** 200

22.
$$\begin{array}{r} 40,000 \\ \times \quad\ .05 \\ \hline 2000.00 \end{array}$$ *Answer:* **(C)** $2000

23. Commission = 42½% of fares
$$42\frac{1}{2}\% \text{ of } \$520 = .425 \times \$520$$
$$= \$221 \text{ commission}$$
Tips = 29% of commission
$$29\% \text{ of } \$221 = .29 \times \$221$$
$$= \$64.09 \text{ tips}$$

Weekly earnings:
$$\begin{array}{r} \$221.00 \\ + \quad 64.09 \\ \hline \$285.09 \end{array}$$

Monthly earnings:
$$\begin{array}{r} \$285.09 \\ \times \qquad 4 \\ \hline \$1140.36 \end{array}$$

Answer: **(C)** between $1100 and $1200

24. *N/15* means the payment is due 15 days from the date of the invoice. Fifteen days from March 18 is April 2.

Answer: **(B)** April 2

25. $300 \times \$.20 = \$ \ 60.00$
  $200 \times \$.13 = \$ \ 26.00$
  $400 \times \$.17 = \underline{\$ \ 68.00}$
  $\hspace{4.8cm}\$154.00$

Answer: **(C)** $154.00

26.
$$\begin{array}{r} \$90.32 \\ 30.82 \\ 7.21 \\ 18.79 \\ 7.25 \\ 1.88 \end{array}$$

Total deductions $\overline{\$156.27}$

$$\begin{array}{rl} \$497.05 & \text{total earnings} \\ \underline{-\ \ 156.27} & \text{deductions} \\ \$340.78 & \text{net pay} \end{array}$$

Answer: **(D)** $340.78

27. If 25% are damaged, then 75% are not damaged.

Type A: 75% of 200 = $.75 \times 200$
  $= 150$
    20% of 150 are wrong color
      20% of 150 = $.20 \times 150$
  $= 30$
Type B: 75% of 100 = $.75 \times 100$
  $= 75$
    40% of 75 are wrong color
      40% of 75 = $.40 \times 75$
  $= 30$
  Total wrong color = 30 + 30 = 60

Answer: **(D)**   60

28. Average is $\dfrac{4000 + 6000}{2} = 5000$ per block

 If there are 60 blocks, there are
  $60 \times 5000 = 300{,}000$ people

 Answer: **(B)** 300,000

29.   1 guilder = \$.3815
  138 guilders = 138(\$.3815)
      = \$52.647

 Answer: **(B)** \$52.65 (to the nearest cent)

30.

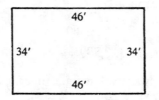

 Perimeter = 46′ + 34′ + 46′ + 34′
        = 160′
 160 ft ÷ 3 ft per yd = $^{160}/_{3}$ yd
        = 53⅓ yd

 Answer: **(D)** 53⅓ yd

31. $\$432 \times 5\frac{3}{4}\% = \cancel{432} \times \overset{}{\underset{100}{^{23}\!/_{\cancel{400}}}}$ $\overset{108}{}$

$$= \$^{2484}\!/_{100}$$
$$= \$24.84$$

$\$74.52 \div \$24.84 = 3$

Answer: **(B)** 3 yr

32. $\$31.29 = 105\%$ of price before tax
Price before tax $= \$31.29 \div 105\%$
$\qquad\qquad\qquad = \$31.29 \div 1.05$
$\qquad\qquad\qquad = \$29.80$

Answer: **(A)** $29.80

33. $\$3515 = 15\%$ of taxable income
Taxable income $= \$2775 \div 15\%$
$\qquad\qquad\qquad = \$2775 \div .15$
$\qquad\qquad\qquad = \$18,500$

Answer: **(A)** $18,500

34. The mode is the value appearing most frequently.
For the list given, the mode is 3.

Answer: **(A)** 3

35. Individual income tax $=\quad 42\%$
Corporate income tax $= \underline{+\ 16\%}$
$\qquad$ Total $\qquad\quad = \quad 58\%$
58% of $352.6 billion $= .58 \times \$352.6$ billion
$\qquad\qquad\qquad\qquad\quad = \$204.508$ billion

Answer: **(C)** 205

36. The total of all of the sectors of the graph except
     excise tax is 94%. Therefore, excise tax revenues
     are 100% − 94%, or 6%.
     6% of $352.6 billion = .06 × $352.6 billion
                          = $21.156 billion

     Answer: **(D)**   21

37. If 37 wear glasses, 100 − 37, or 63 do not wear
     glasses. The probability is $^{63}/_{100}$ = .63

     Answer: **(C)**   .63

38. 60 days = $^{60}/_{360}$ year   Interest = $148 × .06 × ⅙
              = ⅙ year   = $1.48

     Answer: **(D)** $1.48

39. First discount:
           20% of $160 = .20 × $160 = $32
           $160 − $32 = $128
     Second discount:
           10% of $128 = .10 × $128 = $12.80
     $128.00 − $12.80 = $115.20

     Answer: **(B)** $115.20

40.   4 in = ⅓ ft
                                      25
        Volume to be added = 75 × 42 × ⅓

                          = 1050 cu ft
                          = 1050 × 7.58 gal
                          = 7854 gal

     Answer: **(C)**   7854

41. Commission on first $7000:
$$4\tfrac{1}{2}\% \text{ of } \$7000 = .045 \times \$7000$$
$$= \$315$$
Commission on remainder:
$$\$9600 - \$7000 = \$2600$$
$$5\tfrac{1}{2}\% \text{ of } \$2600 = .055 \times \$2600$$
$$= \$143$$

Total commission $= \$315 + \$143$
$$= \$458$$

Answer: **(B)** $458

42. Volume of the carton $= 3 \text{ ft} \times 4 \text{ ft} \times 5 \text{ ft}$
$$= 36 \text{ in} \times 48 \text{ in} \times 60 \text{ in}$$
$$= 103{,}680 \text{ cu in}$$
Volume of each box $= 3 \text{ in} \times 4 \text{ in} \times 5 \text{ in}$
$$= 60 \text{ cu in}$$

$$103{,}680 \div 60 = 1728$$

Answer: **(C)** 1728

43.
32 nickels $=$	$32 \times \$.05 =$	$ 1.60
73 quarters $=$	$73 \times \$.25 =$	18.25
156 dimes $=$	$156 \times \$.10 =$	15.60
	Total $=$	$35.45

Answer: **(C)** $35.45

44. $1855 - 1200 = 655$
The 24-hour clock begins at midnight, therefore
$$1855 = 6:55 \text{ p.m.}$$

Answer: **(B)** 6:55 p.m.

45. $$48 - 40 = 8 \text{ hours overtime}$$
Salary for 8 hours overtime:

$$1\frac{1}{2} \times \$8.60 \times 8 = \frac{3}{2} \times \$8.60 \times \overset{4}{\cancel{8}}$$
$$= \$103.20$$

Salary for 40 hours regular time:
$$\$8.60 \times 40 = \$344.00$$
$$\text{Total salary} = \$344.00 + \$103.20$$
$$= \$447.20$$

Answer: **(A)** $447.20

46. From March 31 to May 15 is 45 days, which is $\frac{45}{360}$ of a year.

$$\text{Interest} = \$200 \times .08 \times \overset{1}{\cancel{\frac{45}{360}}}_{8}$$

$$= \$\frac{16}{8}$$
$$= \$2$$

She must pay $200 + $2 = $202.

Answer: **(B)** $202

47. .57 kilograms $= .57 \times 1000$ grams
$\phantom{.57 \text{ kilograms}} = 570$ grams
$\phantom{.57 \text{ kilograms}} = 570 \div .10$ decigrams
$\phantom{.57 \text{ kilograms}} = 5700$ decigrams

Answer: **(C)** 5700

48. The cost of 5½ dozen is
$$5\frac{1}{2} \times \$1.10 = 5.5 \times \$1.10$$
$$= \$6.05$$

The candies sell at 3 for $.55. A dozen sell for
$4 \times \$.55$, or $2.20. The selling price of 5½ dozen is
$$5½ \times \$2.20 = 5.5 \times \$2.20$$
$$= \$12.10$$
$$\text{Profit} = \$12.10 - \$6.05$$
$$= \$6.05$$

Answer: **(B)** $6.05

49. 1 kg = 2.2 lb
20 kg = 20(2.2) lb
    = 44 lb

Answer: **(C)** 44 pounds

50. Cost + profit = selling price
$$\$16.00 + .35(\$16.00) = \$21.60$$
The selling price of 12 binders is $21.60.
The selling price of 1 binder is
$$\$21.60 \div 12 = \$1.80$$

Answer: **(C)** $1.80

APPENDIX
Tables of Measures

English Measures

Length
1 foot (ft or ') = 12 inches (in or ")
1 yard (yd) = 36 inches
1 yard = 3 feet
1 rod (rd) = 16½ feet
1 furlong = 40 rods
1 mile (mi) = 5280 feet
1 mile = 1760 yards
1 mile = 320 rods

Weight
1 pound (lb) = 16 ounces (oz)
1 hundredweight (cwt) = 100 pounds
1 ton (T) = 2000 pounds
1 long ton = 2240 pounds

Area
1 square foot (ft²) = 144 square inches (in²)
1 square yard (yd²) = 9 square feet

Liquid Measure
1 cup (c) = 8 fluid ounces (fl oz)
1 pint (pt) = 2 cups
1 pint = 4 gills (gi)
1 quart (qt) = 2 pints
1 gallon (gal) = 4 quarts
1 barrel (bl) = 31½ gallons

Dry Measure
1 quart (qt) = 2 pints (pt)
1 peck (pk) = 8 quarts
1 bushel (bu) = 4 pecks

Volume
1 cubic foot (ft³ or cu ft) = 1728 cubic inches
1 cubic yard (yd³ or cu yd) = 27 cubic feet
1 gallon = 231 cubic inches

187

General Measures

Time

1 minute (min) = 60 seconds (sec)
1 hour (hr) = 60 minutes
1 day = 24 hours
1 week = 7 days
1 year = 52 weeks
1 calendar year = 365 days

Angles and Arcs

1 minute (') = 60 seconds (")
1 degree (°) = 60 minutes
1 circle = 360 degrees

Paper Measure

1 quire = 24 sheets
1 ream = 20 quires
1 ream = 480 sheets
1 commercial ream = 500 sheets

Counting

1 dozen (doz) = 12 units
1 gross (gr) = 12 dozen
1 gross = 144 units
1 score = 20 units

Table of English–Metric Conversions (Approximate)

English to Metric

1 inch = 2.54 centimeters
1 yard = .9 meters
1 mile = 1.6 kilometers
1 ounce = 28 grams
1 pound = 454 grams
1 fluid ounce = 30 milliliters
1 liquid quart = .95 liters

Metric to English

1 centimeter = .39 inches
1 meter = 1.1 yards
1 kilometer = .6 miles
1 kilogram = 2.2 pounds
1 liter = 1.06 liquid quart

Table of Metric Conversions*
1 liter = 1000 cubic centimeters (cm³)
1 milliliter = 1 cubic centimeter
1 liter of water weighs 1 kilogram
1 milliliter of water weighs 1 gram

Summary of Geometric Formulas

PERIMETER

Any 2-dimensional figure	P = sum of all the sides
Rectangle	$P = 2(l + w)$
Square	$P = 4s$
Circle	Circumference $= 2\pi r = \pi d$

AREA

Square	$A = s^2$
Rectangle	$A = l \cdot w$
Parallelogram	$A = b \cdot h$
Triangle	$A = \frac{1}{2} \cdot b \cdot h$
Right triangle	$A = \frac{1}{2} \cdot \text{leg}_1 \cdot \text{leg}_2$
Circle	$A = \pi r^2$

VOLUME

Rectangular solid	$V = l \cdot w \cdot h$
Cube	$V = e^3$
Circular cylinder	$V = \pi r^2 h$

---

* These conversions are exact only under specific conditions. If the conditions are not met, the conversions are approximate.

Sphere	$V = \frac{4}{3}\pi r^3$
Cone	$V = \frac{1}{3}\pi r^2 h$
Pyramid	$V = \frac{1}{3} \cdot B \cdot h$
	(B = area of base)

Business Definitions

Accounts receivable: The various amounts of money that a business is due to receive.

Affidavit: A declaration in writing sworn to before a person legally competent to take oaths.

Amortization: The process of gradually repaying a debt or obligation before the time on which it falls due.

Annuity: A sum of money paid yearly for the period of a life.

Asset: Property which may be used in the payment of debts.

Assignee: An individual who receives property or power by transfer from another.

Attorney-in-fact: One who is appointed by another to make contracts for him.

Bank draft: An order from one bank upon another to pay a specified amount, and made payable to a third party. Bank drafts are purchased by the remitter from the originating bank and are endorsed to the remitter's creditor.

Bankrupt: One who has been unable to meet his bills as they fall due and has been declared bankrupt by a court.

Barter: A contract to exchange goods for goods instead of money.

Beneficiary: One who has the profit, benefit, or advantage arising from a contract or an estate.

Bibliography: A list of books relating to a particular subject.

Bilateral contract: A contract where both parties are bound to fulfill obligations reciprocally towards each other.

Bill of exchange: An unconditional order in writing by one person to another signed by the giver, charging the person to whom it was given, to pay on demand or at some future time a certain sum to a specified person.

Bill of lading: A receipt, usually in duplicate or triplicate, of goods received, given by the carrier to the shipper.

Bona fide: In good faith; honestly.

Bond: A specially sealed instrument in writing to secure the payment of money or the performance of an obligation.

Budget: A statement of probable revenue and expenditures and of financial proposals for the ensuing year.

Capital: The money or the principal invested in a business.

Cashier's check: A check drawn by a bank upon itself and signed by the cashier or other authorized officer.

Chattels: Personal and real property.

Certified check: A personal check which has been presented to the bank cashier who has marked it "certified," signed his name, and charged the amount against the drawer's account just as if it had already been paid out. A certified check is guaranteed by the bank. When a person to whose order a check is made out signs his name on the back of the check, i.e., endorses it, the check is payable at the bank to whoever presents it. Checks dated on Sundays or holidays are acceptable at banks.

Chronological: That which pertains to time and the arrangement of events in the order of time.

Close the books: To calculate the income and expenditures of an organization for some specified period.

Codicil: A supplement, adding to, revoking, or explaining something in the body of a will.

Collateral security: Property transferred by the owner to another individual to secure the carrying out of an obligation.

Commercial draft: A form of letter, sent through a bank, from one person to another, requesting that a certain sum of money be paid to the person presenting the letter.

Consign: To send goods to a buyer or to an agent to sell. Payment is made if the goods are sold. If the goods are not sold, the consignee returns the consignments to the consignor.

Contract: A formal agreement between two or more parties. In law a contract is recognized as an obligation to do or not to do a particular thing.

Debenture: A sealed instrument given by a company as security for a loan.

Demurrage: The allowance made by a shipper of goods to the owners of a ship for detaining the ship in port longer than the period agreed upon. The term is also applied to railroads and other forms of transportation.

Discount: To buy or accept for less than face value, the difference going to the purchaser. The amount deducted is called a discount.

Dividend: A portion of the earnings of a corporation distributed on a percentage basis to holders of stock in proportion to number or par value of shares held.

Endorse: To write one's name on the back of negotiable paper for the purpose of transferring title and guaranteeing payment.

Escrow: A sealed instrument given by one party to another to deliver to a third person when that third person performs a certain act or acts. It is in force until delivered to that third party.

Estimate: A statement of the probable cost of work to be done or goods to be purchased.

Executor: One appointed by the terms of a will to carry out the provisions of that will.

Facsimile: An exact copy.

Factor: An agent employed to sell merchandise for a compensation called a "factorage" or "commission."

Foreclosure: A court action by which a mortgagor is banned from the redemption of his property and thereby loses it.

Franchise: The right sold by a manufacturer to a distributor to market the manufacturer's brand-name product or service for a percentage of the profits.

Indemnity: That which is given in payment for a loss or damage.

Inventory: A detailed account, catalog, or schedule of possessions. An organization will take an inventory in order to know what merchandise it has on hand.

Invoice: A list sent to the purchaser containing the items, together with the prices and charges, of merchandise sent or to be sent to him.